CHOICES

One person's journey out of homosexuality

Christopher Keane

ACORN PRESS

Published by Acorn Press Ltd, ABN 50 008 549 540
Office and orders:
PO Box 282
Brunswick East
Victoria 3057
Australia
Tel/Fax (03) 9383 1266
International Tel/Fax 61 3 9383 1266
Website: www.acornpress.net.au

National Library of Australia Cataloguing-in-Publication entry

Author:	Keane, Christopher.
Title:	Choices : one person's journey out of homosexuality / Christopher Keane.
ISBN:	9780908284757 (pbk.)
Subjects:	Keane, Christopher. Christian biography--Australia. Ex-gays--Australia--Biography. Homosexuality--Religious aspects--Christianity.
Dewey Number:	248.2092

Grateful acknowledgement is given to Harvest House Publishers, for permission to reprint a selection from When *Homosexuality Hits Home*, by Joe Dallas (copyright © 2004); to Ignatius Press, for permission to reprint a selection from *The Battle for Normality: A Guide for (Self-) Therapy for Homosexuality*, by Gerard van den Aardweg (copyright © 1997); and to Matthias Media, for permission to reprint a selection from *What Some of You Were: Stories about Christians and Homosexuality*, by Chris Keane (ed.) (copyright © 2001).

Cover design and text layout: Les Colston www.zealart.com.au
Printed by: Openbook Howden, Adelaide.

To Truda

Other books by Christopher Keane *et al.*

What Some of You Were – Stories about Christians and Homosexuality

CONTENTS

ACKNOWLEDGEMENTS

Firstly I want to acknowledge and thank the many men and women who have shared their stories and their struggles with us. Thank you for your trust. We have always respected your courage and perseverance and it has been a privilege to be a part of your journey.

In order to protect the identities of some people mentioned in this book, names have been changed.

Thank you to the many friends who have encouraged me in the writing of this book. It's not possible to list you all here, but you know who you are.

Finally, thank you to Bishop Ken and Mrs Gloria Short for your love, friendship, prayers and support given so generously, firstly to Truda and then to both of us over many, many years.

INTRODUCTION

Our choices make our future.

During our lives we are faced with many choices. We are also faced with the consequences of those choices. The choices may vary from the simple, like what to wear, to the more important, for example, how we choose to live our life. I didn't make a deliberate choice to be attracted sexually to men. I very much doubt *anyone* chooses to be homosexual. But I did make the choice to *live* as an active homosexual for fifteen years.

In time, I found it to be a destructive and unhappy experience. Realising that homosexuality hadn't worked for me, I decided to leave it and to try and live my life by the standards God has revealed in the Bible. I have absolutely no regrets about my choice, as it has brought me happiness, contentment, and spiritual, emotional, and sexual fulfilment.

The Christian church is now divided on the issue of homosexuality. Some sections of the church want to legitimise homosexuality by both ordaining practising homosexuals and 'marrying' or 'blessing' same-sex couples. On the other side of the fence the more bigoted Christians march against homosexuals, condemning them. Neither of these extremes will do. Many within the Christian community are in a state of confusion about what the Christian attitude to homosexuality should be, and some have given up entirely on the issue because they find it all too hard.

Some people who struggle with same-sex attraction have been hurt by the insensitive attitudes of a minority of Christians with very misinformed views about homosexuality, as well as by the ignorance that surrounds homosexuality in general. In fact, some have been so hurt that they are quite antagonistic to both Christians and Christianity. Sadly, some even see God through the filter of misinformed Christians who have inflicted their unhelpful views on them. Scratch the surface of some Christians, and underneath there is often an entrenched, but unfounded, belief that homosexuality really is the worst sin of all.

My aim in writing this book is to tell the story of how I broke with a sexually active homosexual life, as well as the process of change I experienced after I left that life.

I wasn't seeking change; I wouldn't have thought change was possible until it began to happen to me. My experience has been that, as what I consider to be contributing factors of my homosexual condition were dealt with, a significant measure of change occurred in my sexuality. I am not saying this happens for all, but it has happened for me.

Over time many people have asked me how they can best help other Christians who struggle with unwanted same-sex attraction. So as well as my own story, I have included information about what one can do if they have a homosexual friend or relative.

My hope and prayer is that as you read this book you will clearly see the love, the gentleness, and the incredibly caring way in which God has worked in my life – a life that was very broken. I offer this book as a testimony to a love that is available to all, from a God who cares for all.

Christopher Keane

The small boy slipped into the church away from the noise of the playground. It was quiet in here. It was also better than watching the other kids who were occupied with their own games and friends. They all seemed to have others to run around with but he didn't.

It didn't matter in here though. The church was quiet and he felt at peace. He could smell the furniture polish they used on the seats. He liked that smell. He also liked the statues and the little red light that glowed up near the front of the church. The noise of the playground receded and he let the quietness wash over him.

He had asked Mumma about God. She said that God was everywhere and could see everyone, and that he knew all about them. That answer satisfied him because he had never doubted that God existed and he found it a comfort to know that he was everywhere and saw everything. He also knew that this place had something to do with God but he was too little to work out what it was. He just knew that he felt at peace here.

Was he reaching for God ... or was God reaching for him?

CHAPTER 1

The Other Side of the Rainbow

'A person has to get fed up with the ways of the world before he, before she, acquires an appetite for the world of grace.'

Eugene H Peterson, *The Journey*[1]

Who knows, perhaps the beginning of the end started for me as I stood in the bar and prayed. Here I was in my early thirties, healthy, financially comfortable, with an excellent job, living in one of Sydney's best and most beautiful suburbs, and none of it really mattered because all I felt was lonely and miserable.

I stood watching the crowd in the small wine bar. It was a mixture of young, well dressed, and mostly, good-looking men. Enzo's – as the bar was called – was located in Paddington, one of the eastern suburbs of Sydney where many gays lived. It was small, L-shaped around the bar and softly lit. The air was full of cigarette smoke and the conflicting aromas of the various colognes and aftershaves being worn. Some of the men who frequented the bar had a look of quiet desperation about them. They were looking for Mr Right, but most were happy to settle for Mr Anyone. During the week there were enough people to make it interesting, but on Friday and Saturday nights the bar was packed.

There was a jukebox which was never silent, continuously pumping out a selection of the latest music. Out the back was a small garden which had several tables and chairs and where, on a warm night, it was pleasant to sit. However, if one hoped to meet someone it was best to stay inside, as that was where the majority of people drank and socialised. I would have classed myself as one of the regulars, as I drank there at least two or three nights a week. The nights started out with a sense of expectation. There was always the hope that this would be the night when the 'right' person would appear. It was desperate and sad.

During the time I was involved in the gay community, the drinking and socialising scene had undergone many changes. Sydney had changed and had become more cosmopolitan, and homosexuality was now certainly more 'out there'. I could remember when there had been only a couple of hotels where one could go to meet other gays. Homosexuality became more blatant, as well as more vocal and socially acceptable, and now there were many more bars and pubs in Sydney which catered to the gay community. Each had its own character and each attracted a certain type of homosexual. There were some bars and hotels where the clientele was rougher and more 'blokey' than others, just as there were bars that attracted the more conservative, middle class homosexual. There were also bars that catered for the lesbian population of Sydney.

There were gay nightclubs such as The Purple Onion and Capriccio's, which had floorshows. Some of the drag queens who performed in these places were extremely clever and creative; they had a large following of people, including many heterosexuals.

From time to time tastes would change and where one bar would be popular for a while, the clientele would then move on to somewhere different. Even back then the pink dollar had a lot of power and the gay community was quite capricious in its choices.

This had happened with the Purple Onion. I remember Sunday nights at the Onion were a 'must' for the crowd I moved with. It was a great way to end the weekend. After spending two days at the beach working on our suntans and after the big night out on Saturday, we would end up at the Onion for the Sunday night floorshow. We all looked good – or thought we did – with our tanned bodies, tight trousers and our hair blow-dried to within an inch of its life. In time this venue lost its popularity and Capriccio's became the more popular place. Later the Purple Onion was converted into a gay sauna.

The vocabulary had also changed. Where once homosexuals had called themselves 'camp', somewhere along the way they had adopted and now used the word 'gay' – a word which surely has to be the misnomer of the age.

I had been part of the Sydney gay community for about twelve years.

During that time I had had three long-term relationships and some short-term ones, all of which ended in disappointment and hurt. I had never taken the time to work through the pain involved in these break-ups. I was immediately out there again looking, always with the hope that maybe the next relationship would be the one that would last. This was fairly typical behaviour among the people I knew.

After many years I had become very dissatisfied and disillusioned with my life, and in particular the homosexual community in which I moved.

When I first became involved in homosexuality in my teens, it had appeared to be exciting and full of promise. It was all new, and after being aware from a young age of my sexual attraction to other men, it was a relief to be in places where other homosexual people met.

I was initiated into both the sexual and the social aspects of homosexuality through someone I met in my local church. I had become a Christian at sixteen and had started going to a local church. I was growing as a Christian and had a deep and sincere desire to know God. I studied the Bible, prayed, and read voraciously – especially Christian biographies. I was hungry for God and was steadily growing closer to him. The whole experience was wonderful. Although I knew I was sexually attracted to other men, it wasn't something I would have even considered discussing with anyone in my church. There was a great deal of shame connected with homosexuality at that time and it wasn't something I was going to come out about anywhere, let alone in church. Also, in many ways I was a private person and my sexuality was one of the areas I would never have considered talking about with anyone.

An older man transferred to our church from another state and he was included in a small group of us from the church who had been going out together for a while. As I got to know this man I realised there was an attraction between us and it wasn't long before a relationship began. There was an excitement and a relief for me in this, as the years of being sexually attracted to men and the desire for same-sex affection and sex now had a focus and an outlet.

I started spending a great deal of time with Richard. I would stay at his apartment on weekends and we would go to the beach or a film together, or sometimes just stay home and listen to music. I was sixteen, he was twenty-eight. Although many would probably see this as abuse of a minor, I was a willing participant. The affection I was receiving from an older man was very heady and addictive stuff for a time.

I knew what the Bible said about homosexuality, so for me, Christianity and active homosexuality were never going to be compatible. As I saw it, I had three choices I could have made. I could have fought the temptation and continued as a Christian; I could have gone into the relationship and continued to attend church whilst keeping what we were doing secret; or I could have made the choice to leave God right out of the picture and become involved with Richard, which is what I did. It saddens me now when I look back and see how quickly I deserted God. Close to him one day and gone the next.

Strangely enough, this didn't create any emotional conflict for me at the time. The reason for this may have been that I had finally found what I had been craving for so many years – a sexual and emotional relationship with someone of the same sex. The excitement of this as well as the anticipation of a future together probably blotted out any sense of guilt. I was also very immature in my walk and relationship with God and I certainly had no idea of the spiritual and long-term consequences of what I was doing. Even so, I had made my choice and I was responsible for that choice.

I can't remember Richard and me ever discussing Christianity in the light of our relationship. I don't know if he felt guilty about what we were doing, or perhaps we just avoided the topic because we realised deep down it was a potential minefield that was safer to stay away from.

Even though I had attended this church for some time, no one there questioned the relationship between Richard and me. Neither did anyone follow me up when I stopped attending church.

Richard shared his apartment with another gay man who had several friends who fascinated me. They were witty, enjoyable to be with, and would tell me the most interesting and outrageous stories of where they had been and what they had been doing. It all sounded very exciting and I longed to be a part of it. One of them was a singer and appeared in many of the musical productions in Sydney at that time. Because they were so interesting I loved to spend time with them, but Richard wasn't happy about this at all. They were part of the much larger homosexual community in Sydney which Richard didn't want us to get involved in. He was very protective and did his best to discourage my budding friendship with these men.

At first I found his 'protectiveness' flattering, but in time I found that it was becoming stifling. I suppose, looking back, it was his insecurity that caused him to be the way he was. Anyway, he was fighting a losing battle. I wanted to find out as much as I could about what was 'out there', and I did.

My relationship with Richard ended eventually, and with the help of his flatmate's friends I was introduced to the bar and pub scene that was part of the gay culture in Sydney at that time.

I was still under the age where I could drink in a hotel legally but that didn't stop me. At first I felt very excited to be part of this new world. Instead of feeling I had to *hide* my homosexuality, it was now a relief to be with this group where I fitted in because I *was* homosexual. I was new on the scene, so I had no trouble meeting sexual partners.

This excitement lasted for several years. As I moved out of my teens and into my twenties I still felt the homosexual community was the ultimate in sophistication. I met people whom I viewed with a touch of awe. In most cases these were older men who had done well professionally. I was very much into what was current in fashion as well as the latest in theatre and film, and I went to restaurants and to places I had not been exposed to before. I had been introduced to a very different world to the one in which I had been raised, and it was seductive and an adventure to be a part of it.

Of course, after living this life for many years the excitement I had initially felt had well and truly worn off. I had used people and been used by them, and I had seen and experienced much that had made me very cynical about the life I was living.

So here I was, many wasted years later, standing in a smoke-filled gay bar in Paddington, Sydney, pondering my past and yearning for what I still didn't have – that illusive, life-long relationship.

The bar was beginning to fill up now, so I pushed my way through the crowd to buy another drink. There were people whom I knew, but I didn't want to get involved with them. After greeting them briefly and arming myself with a fresh drink, I moved back to where I had been standing and continued to think about my past relationships.

I met my second serious 'partner' in another bar. I remembered it was a Saturday night and I was drinking with a group of friends when someone from another group came up to me and said 'There's a guy over here who wants to meet you'. I was introduced to Jon and although I was polite I wasn't all that interested in him. After we talked for a while, he disappeared to buy some wine as he was having a few people back to his apartment for drinks. In those days the hotels in Sydney closed at 10 pm. If there was no invitation to someone's apartment for coffee or drinks, those of us who lived with our families had no alternative but to call it a night and go home.

A small group of us ended up back at Jon's place and over the course of the night I got to know him a little. He was an outgoing, happy-go-lucky and confident sort of guy and nothing seemed to worry him. He was a chef, and a very good one, and had moved to Sydney from Melbourne. He made it obvious that he was interested in me and, mainly at his initiative, over the next few weeks we spent more and more time together. As I got to know him better I grew to value and even to miss him when he wasn't around. It didn't take long before I was as keen on him as he was on me.

In time Jon and I decided to live together. This was exciting for me, as I had gone from apathy toward this man to now believing I had met 'the one'. Both of us felt our relationship was going to last forever.

Over time we built up a small group of mutual friends, many of whom were other homosexual couples. Our closest friends, David and Ben, had been together longer than us. These two men lived just around the corner from us and we saw a great deal of them. We went out together, entertained each other for meals, and at times went away together for weekends.

We also knew a great deal about each other. Jon and I knew that Ben was very promiscuous and was having sex with other men without David's knowledge. Although we would never have told David what we knew, it was difficult watching Ben's behaviour knowing that in time it was inevitable that the truth would come out.

This type of unfaithfulness was very common among the couples we knew. Some relationships had developed into long-term friendships, the couples continuing to live together while finding sex outside of the relationship. Some had an unspoken understanding where there were no questions asked of the other person's movements. This was a sort of denial where the attitude seemed to be 'what I don't know won't hurt me'. Others were open about their promiscuity and unfaithfulness to each other. However, Ben was trying hard to keep his promiscuity a secret from David. As David had a huge emotional investment in Ben, I watched what was happening with a great deal of concern. Also, there was always the risk of Ben passing onto him some sort of sexually transmitted disease.

Although this was all happening in the background, Jon and I were still very much enjoying our relationship. We had a great deal in common and we were enlarging our circle of friends. We partied, wined and dined, went to the latest shows and, for a time, there was little to mar our friendship. However, as good as things seemed to be on the surface, I knew deep down from what I had seen amongst most other homosexual couples, that what was happening to David could just as easily happen to me.

The four of us had planned to go to the beach together one Sunday. Jon and I drove around to Ben and David's apartment to pick them up and as we came to their door we could hear David yelling at Ben. The door burst open and David pushed past us and ran out of the building. Ben came to the door, motioned for us to come in, and said 'He's found out'. We didn't need to ask what he'd found out. We had been waiting for the inevitable to happen for some time.

We spent the rest of the day looking for David. Eventually, much later that afternoon, he returned to the apartment. He didn't tell us where he had been nor would he talk about what had happened, so we never knew how he felt. Even though their relationship continued, it had now become one of the many where no questions were asked.

Over time it became clear to me that Jon was also being unfaithful. I had been suspicious but hadn't wanted to admit it to myself. I felt helpless and angry, but mostly very, very hurt. It was such a betrayal, and I found it incredibly difficult to accept and then to process this type of hurt. Even though I had been surrounded by other couples who were incapable or unwilling to practice faithfulness, this was now happening to me, and it was a very different thing to experience this hurt personally rather than just watch someone else go through it.

Finally, after it had been confronted and as I was not prepared to live as David and Ben and many others lived, I moved out into a small apartment on my own. I could see no point in being in a relationship which was devoid of emotional and sexual fidelity.

I thought the pain would never end. In fact I even wondered if I was having some sort of an emotional breakdown. For days at a time I would coast along absolutely numb, but then something would set off the intense feelings of desolation, loss and pain and down I would go once more into despair and depression. I had invested everything in this man and I was now realising that what I had thought of as a life-long commitment had really been just a big lie.

But there was more involved than the grief of a broken relationship. I was also now beginning to face the possibility that this was what the rest of my life was going to be like.

I finally went to a gay doctor I knew to see if he could help me in some way. He listened, looked at me with contempt, and then said, 'Grow up; everyone should have the freedom to play around if that's what they want. To think differently is just plain naive and childish.' He went on, 'If you had any commonsense you would have accepted things as they were and just continued in the relationship. It's better to have someone on those terms than not to have them at all.'

Well, so much for care and understanding.

Neither Jon nor I could make a clean and final break with each other. Even though we both became involved with other people sexually, we still saw each other and continued to sleep together on occasions. It was a messy and painful end to the relationship and, of course, it was impossible to deal with the feelings as we wouldn't let go of each other.

Jon finally met someone he liked enough to live with and moved in with him, and we gradually saw less of each other. I also met someone, and we entered into a relationship although it didn't last for long.

The result of the hurt I felt from this failed relationship was that I hardened myself in an attempt to never feel this type of pain again. I also became very promiscuous and a much more cynical person. I didn't trust people, expected nothing from them, and was also not prepared to give much either.

I am aware some people reading this may be shocked to realise that the break-up of a homosexual relationship can cause the same pain as the break-up of a heterosexual relationship. This may be because some do not see homosexuals as people with the same feelings, needs and reactions as anyone else, but the simple fact is, they are.

My mother died, and when her estate was settled I bought my own apartment. I also changed my job and did very well in the new position. After a short time I was asked to join the staff training section. From there I was promoted to the recruitment section where I was made responsible for the selection and recruitment of the Sydney staff.

One would think I had everything that made for a happy life, and according to my friends, I did. But I felt empty, lonely, and for much of the time, depressed. I was drinking heavily and I was also using marijuana regularly. I missed God and I even prayed sometimes. But I knew I needed more than the occasional prayer when I was feeling desperate. I needed to come back to God. I also knew the life I was living was not at all satisfactory, but at that stage I was unwilling to do anything about it.

I still thought the answer to all my problems was another relationship, and the push to find that 'special' person was something that kept driving me on. It was a futile attempt to fill the vacuum and relieve the emptiness.

This was what my life had become. What had once been exciting and, I had imagined, full of promise had slowly, over many years, been exposed as shallow. It had become for me a pathetic, lonely and sad way of life.

As I stood in the bar that night, I took another long look around me at the sea of faces, and prayed, 'God, just give me one more chance at a relationship and if it doesn't work out this time I'll come back to you.'

CHAPTER 2

At Home with the Keanes

'There is no such thing, strictly speaking, as a homosexual or a lesbian. There are only people who need healing of old rejections and deprivations.'
Leanne Payne[2]

No parent is perfect and no family is perfect. Some people delight in placing all blame for their problems at their parents' feet, thus absolving themselves from taking responsibility for their own lives. Of course my parents didn't deliberately set out to cause me harm, although I believe many of the causes of my homosexuality had their beginnings in my early childhood.

Bringing up a child is not easy when the parents haven't had healthy role models themselves. My parents did the best they could for all their children, but the fact remains, we did suffer from the environment we grew up in.

It's hard to look back after so many years and try to work out 'causes', when childhood memories have been softened by adult insights and much forgiveness has been received and given. What was due to my upbringing? What consequences did my own sinful choices have in my life? What were the ongoing effects of my early childhood abuse? What was *reality* and what were *my perceptions* of reality? And what just 'was' because it 'was'? All the ingredients go into the mix and I don't know if they can be separated out for a closer look, but I'm going to try.

McMahon's Point, when I was growing up, was a working class suburb. Years later it became a much sought-after place to live with its quaint houses, smart restaurants and proximity to the city.

At the bottom of a hill and close to the water, stand – and still do at the time of writing – an old terrace of five houses; we lived in the middle house. It was typical of its time, consisting of three rooms downstairs and two upstairs. The laundry, bathroom and toilet were outside. I slept on a veranda that had been enclosed and was off the main bedroom.

The household was made up of my father, my mother, and my sisters who were twins. I had an older brother, but I didn't meet him until he came back from overseas where he had been living for many years.

I had been an unexpected, and I'm told unwanted, child who came along late in my parents' marriage.

My sisters tell me Mum was so ashamed of being pregnant so long after she had her other children that she cried for the first six months of the pregnancy. As my sisters were fifteen years older than me, and my brother two years older than them, I did most of my growing up in an adult world. My sisters had both wanted a girl and they were very disappointed when I was born and they were told I was a boy.

My father was one of two children, the other child being a girl. His parents' marriage failed very early and they separated. Later when Dad was seven, his father, who was thirty-one, died of tuberculosis. As Dad's mother couldn't manage both children, Dad was sent to live with his paternal grandmother and aunts to be raised by them. With this background, it was no wonder he knew little or nothing of being able to be a father to his own children.

None of his children knew him, and as a child there were times when I was afraid of him. Although he provided for us as a family and was neither violent nor abusive, we were unable to get close to him. I can never remember him showing me any physical affection. I was certainly never held or kissed by him, and apart from the briefest of conversations, I can't remember talking to him on any subject that revealed anything of his personality, tastes, or even his views. He was a complete mystery to me, but one I felt I needed to view from a safe distance. I always felt he was disappointed and vaguely angry with me, but I was never able to understand what I had done to deserve his disappointment. In a perfect world a father would help his son to separate from his mother, affirm him in his gender, and even model to him the more masculine things that would be normal for a boy to learn. If Dad had made an effort and shown interest in me, as well as a little warmth, I would have felt more like spending time with him. Perhaps then a closer relationship may have had the chance of developing, but this just didn't happen.

The fear and uneasiness I felt towards my Dad pushed me more in the direction of my mother. If I confided in anyone, it was to her. She was the one who was always there and who I felt accepted by.

My mother was the second of five children and she was born in the historic area of Sydney called Miller's Point, which was one of the earliest places to be settled in Sydney.

Her mother worked at the Palisade Hotel as a housemaid. She knew the locals as well as their stories. I'm told she used to sit on a step outside the hotel in her breaks and gossip to the locals. When she was twenty-four Nan met my grandfather, who was eighteen, and they were married. She always maintained he was a very mature man, and I'm told he was very good looking. Although they managed to have five children, apparently it wasn't a very happy marriage. Nan was the only grandparent I knew as the others had all died by the time I was born.

My mother inherited much of my grandmother's gregariousness and humour, and could be extremely funny and very outgoing when she chose. However, probably because of her lack of formal education, she was a very insecure woman. This insecurity was something which affected us in our socialising, as we were not allowed to bring any of our friends home. She always felt self-conscious about the house we lived in, although when I compared it with some of my school friends' homes, there was nothing wrong with it. She was also extremely sensitive; at times she imagined put-downs and slights from people when there were, in reality, probably none. She was twenty when she married Dad, he was twenty-two.

There was often a feeling of tension in our home. Mum's sensitivity frequently overflowed onto others, and at times we walked around as if we were treading on eggshells. As a child I never really figured it all out, I just knew the atmosphere had an underlying tension at times.

There was also a lot of noise in our home. Because Dad was hard of hearing, the radio – and later the television – was always loud. People also spoke loudly so he could hear. The constant shouting and noise, as well as the tension that was often present, affected me, and for much of the time I was tense.

Fear was also a big part of my growing up. When I started to go out at night as a young adult, I was always warned about the danger of being bashed or murdered if I failed to 'get a taxi home'. The stories of people who had been attacked or murdered were always dragged out and used as examples of what could happen to me if I wasn't careful. Although these warnings were meant well, all they succeeded in doing was to engender fear in me.

Sometime during the Second World War, and before I was born, the entire family had moved from Miller's Point to McMahon's Point on the other side of Sydney Harbour. My grandfather, grandmother, uncles and aunt moved to the top of the hill; Dad, Mum and our family moved down the bottom.

My uncle Leslie – Mum's brother – was the main male influence I had as a child. I can remember that he always seemed to be available in emergencies. He was like my mother in that he was a fairly insecure person, but they both shared a wonderful sense of humour. He seemed to think life owed him a living and was always envious of others who were better off than he was. Nevertheless, I loved him. I remember him taking me out to interesting places, and he was often in our home. Of all her siblings, I think this brother was Mum's favourite. Many years later after I had grown up he told me he was gay.

But life wasn't all grim. I had many happy times growing up. Before the days of television I loved listening to the serials on our big radio in the living room. I can't remember all of them, but Superman was one of my favourites. We also used to listen regularly to Jack Davey's and Bob Dyer's quiz shows. On Sunday night there was always a radio play which we enjoyed, and then I went off to bed so I wouldn't be too tired for school the next day.

My love of reading started at a very early age. I read just about anything and everything, but I had several favourite authors. Enid Blyton was one I remember vividly, and I could think of nothing better than getting stuck into a new book, especially a new Blyton book. The 'Famous Five' books and her mystery series were amongst my favourites. I just loved the fact that these groups of children had the company and friendship of each other, and I suppose I was envious of that.

I was also often taken to the movies, and grew up in the time when the Metro-Goldwyn-Mayer musicals were at their height. It was a great escape for an hour or two, as Judy Garland, Fred Astaire, Gene Kelly or Debbie Reynolds sang and danced their way across the screen. We all knew everything was going to turn out OK by the end of the film, and the inevitable happy ending usually came either just before or just after the big production number. Ah yes, life was simple at MGM!

Our neighbours were an interesting lot. On our right lived a gentle, quietly spoken and very reserved English woman. Mrs Langton was her name, but I called her Lang. The toilets for each house in our terrace were down the bottom of the backyard; ours and our neighbour's were semi-detached and only divided by a wall. If both neighbours were in the 'loo' at the same time, there was little or no privacy. As a small child this didn't faze me at all, but I'm sure I caused dear Mrs Langton no end of embarrassment. If I heard her in the toilet I would yell out to her 'Is that you, Lang?' – I don't know who else it would have been as she lived alone! Her reply was usually a very quiet 'M'mm'. Having elicited some response, however slight, I would then proceed to chatter on to her about this and that, including what was happening in my day. All of this happened with very little, if any, comment from her. I could never understand why she wasn't very communicative at these times.

Mrs Langton had a huge Alsatian dog called Jacko. This animal was the terror of my life. Lang would sometimes invite me in to her house, but it was always something of a mixed blessing. I loved her North Country accent, and she used to give me drinks of her lemon cordial. These things were great attractions to me, but I was in a continuous state of nervousness because I was so afraid of her dog.

The neighbour on our left was Mrs Boyd, whom we called Boydie. She was a kind and very pleasant lady, and she and my mother were very friendly. They used to talk most days over the back fence, where they kept each other up to date on the 'doings' of the neighbourhood.

The lady who lived next door to Mrs Boyd – two doors down from us – was Mrs Potter. She kept us all amused as she was forever mixing up her words. Hysterectomy became 'hyster-requiem'. Fictitious became 'fastidious'. Someone had suffered a 'coronary occasion', and so on. One day she confused my mother by telling her about the 'awful Lebanese women' who worked with a friend of hers. Mum asked her what was wrong with Lebanese women. She lowered her voice and replied, 'Really Mrs Keane, it's too awful to talk about.' My mother must have looked bewildered by this, so Mrs Potter continued, 'You know, homosexigan women ... lebaneses!'

I really loved these neighbours. Our terrace was something of a small community, where we would call on each other for help in emergencies. I regret that after I moved away from McMahon's Point I didn't keep in touch with them.

My brother returned from overseas but died two months before my sixth birthday. He was injured in a fight, admitted to hospital where he remained for a while, but didn't recover from his injuries.

Dad, on his way to the hospital to visit my brother, had slipped and broken his kneecap. He was hospitalised, and my brother died while Dad was still an inpatient. A neighbour told me years later that as they were on their way to the cemetery, the funeral procession passed the hospital and Dad was standing on the veranda, waving. She said it was one of the saddest things she had ever seen.

My brother's death was never explained to me in a way I could understand or accept as a six-year-old. I was told he was dead and never coming back, but we were not going to talk about it. Finish and close of subject. I found out the details after I had grown up.

Not only was my Dad emotionally distant and detached, he was also a very passive man. One day, when I was about three or four, I was taken by my mother and father to visit my father's sister. She was married to an alcoholic, a man the whole family feared. I can remember my uncle sitting me on his knee and proceeding to interfere with me. He put his hand down my shorts and forced his finger into my back passage. I was scared and in pain, but too frightened to move. I badly wanted someone to make him stop and take me away from him. What is incredible to me, as I look back on this incident, was the fact that my mother, father and aunt were all present in the room and in plain view of my uncle and me. I assume they knew what was happening, but none of them did anything to stop him. These were the people who should have been my protectors.

I also experienced another sexual assault as a child when visiting my uncle Leslie. He deliberately and inappropriately exposed himself to me. I would have been about seven or eight at that time. He was my favourite uncle, and this event altered my relationship with him. For many years this man had been a positive and loving part of my life, and I trusted him and loved him very much. Now I was confused by what he had done. By exposing himself, he had altered our relationship and my feelings toward him changed. I now felt that I didn't really know him and didn't know what to expect from him anymore. I was confused. My trust had gone. Everything was different, and because I didn't know how to cope with the way I now felt about him, I avoided him. He was lost to me, and I felt sad about that and missed him. I never told anyone about what had happened to me that day.

Some people may think that describing these events as child sexual assault may be too strong, but the former New South Wales Child Protection Council defined child sexual assault in the following way:

> Child sexual assault occurs when an adult or someone bigger than a child uses his power or authority over the child and takes advantage of the child's trust and respect to involve the child in sexual activity.
>
> Child sexual assault does not refer only to sexual intercourse, although sexual intercourse is often involved. Child sexual assault includes fondling genitals, masturbation, oral sex, vaginal or anal penetration by a finger, penis, or any other object. It may also include exhibitionism and suggestive behaviour. In all cases, the offender has more power than the child and misuses that power to take advantage of the child.[3]

I was having a bad run with the men in my life. My father was emotionally distant, which made it impossible for me to know him, and I often felt afraid of him. Just when I was getting to know my older brother, he died. One uncle had abused me; another uncle had exposed himself to me, and so I became very wary of him. There were no other men around me to whom I felt close. I think it was probably about this time that I completely gave up on men. I concluded that it was all just too hard, so I stopped trying to relate to *any* men. They were a mystery, and although they held a strong fascination and attraction for me, I had had no positive relationship with any man at all.

As I grew older, I began to fantasise over some of my teachers and various other men I saw. These were always men who had strong personalities and were very masculine in appearance. My fantasy usually involved them looking after me or protecting me in some way. Later, when I entered puberty, these fantasies became sexualised. I suppose one doesn't have to be too sharp to see the 'father hunger' that was present in the fantasies, but I didn't recognise it for what it was until many years later.

Although I was short on the healthy influence of men in my life, what *was* available were three strong women. But no matter how loving they were – and they *were* very loving – they were no substitute for a father or father figure.

I thought my older sisters were the most glamorous creatures alive. They made their own clothes, and I used to watch fascinated, as they created beautiful dresses from paper patterns and lengths of material. I learned to value creativity from them and, as there was no male model around, I modelled on them and tried to emulate them in many ways. They spent time with me, and I learned from them things that were traditionally classed as female pastimes.

Often they would take me to the city on a Saturday to shop. I loved this particular outing because they took me to all the big stores. I can still vividly remember coming down the escalators in David Jones' department store and the wonderful smells from the perfume department on the ground floor enveloping me. It was all very mysterious and adult, and very exciting to be a part of it. My sisters took an interest in me and gave me lots of affection. In my eyes they were everything that was sophisticated, and I wanted to be as much like them as I could.

They had a special girlfriend, Jane, who was the only person to stay overnight at our home. This was usually on a Saturday night after the three had been out dancing at the Trocadero. The 'Troc' – as many people called it – was a Sydney institution in those days and held a dance on Saturday and Sunday nights. Jane would keep us all amused as she recounted tales of the characters they had met or danced with. She had outrageous names for all the regulars and would describe them for us over breakfast on Sunday mornings. Looking back, I realise that both my sisters, as well as Jane, all met the men they married at the 'Troc'.

If they didn't go to the dance on a Saturday night, but instead had a date with some guy for a movie, there would always be the leftovers of a box of chocolates for me to scrounge the next day.

Although there were other neighbourhood children who were the same age as me and with whom I sometimes mixed, much of my growing up was done surrounded by adults, whom I thought were much more interesting than the kids I occasionally played with. This contributed to my being mainly content to be a loner, and by the time I had reached high school this pattern was well and truly entrenched.

I can never remember experiencing any encouragement at home. I was never told I was good at anything, nor was I encouraged in any hobby or interest. I was never made to feel that I was adequate or competent in any way. At the time, I thought this was normal, but I later came to see that it is a very normal thing for children to be encouraged by their parents. The overwhelming feeling I experienced was that everyone at home, and in particular my father, were all slightly ashamed of me.

School was a lonely and painful time of my life. Although I had some close friendships, there was a lot of name-calling or 'labelling' – poofter, pansy, queer – as I was effeminate and different from most of the other boys. This was not very surprising, considering that I had not had a healthy masculine role model in my family and had instead modelled myself on my sisters.

For me, school was also a place of rejection as I just didn't fit in. I was sensitive and spent a great deal of my time battling the rejection of my peers. This rejection fed into my already well-established habit of protecting myself from pain. I began to spend more and more time with either my nose in a book or at the movies – after all, it was safer and much more pleasant to be involved in that world, than to be part of a world where I was called names and didn't fit in. Of course, this caused me to isolate myself even more from my peer group. The few friends I did make at school were kids like me, who didn't fit into the 'A' group or had been marginalised for some other reason.

I particularly loathed high school, and the part I loathed the most was the period called Physical Education. We had a P.E. teacher who was a very good-looking man, and I had a crush on this teacher for all of my years at high school. Many years later I found out that he was gay. I hated being in his class, though. I can remember the thing I really dreaded about P.E. was the vaulting horse. I never learned to master this monster, but would love to have been let loose on it in private with an axe!

Instead of enjoying adolescence, I was just waiting to grow up, all the time looking forward to the freedom I thought being an adult would bring. I thought that freedom had arrived on the day I turned 15. I had decided that enough was enough. I went to the headmaster, told him I was leaving, and then I just walked out.

This created a huge drama at home as I hadn't told my parents I intended leaving. They wanted me to go on and get the Intermediate Certificate, which at that time was the equivalent of the School Certificate. There was no way I was going back to school, and so I cried and cried until I gradually wore my parents down and they finally accepted the fact that school was over for me. I have never regretted my decision to leave, although there have been times when not having any formal educational qualification has proved to be a disadvantage.

One of my first jobs was a clerical position in a large company on the

North Shore. It was a great job and one that I enjoyed. I made friends with two women who worked in the same company. They were much older than me, but we got along well so age was unimportant. One of the places I loved to go with these women was to an Italian restaurant near home that had a small band. We danced to Latin American music, drank Italian wine, and I thought this was the very pinnacle of sophistication.

It was about this time that a friend introduced me to his older sister. One day, while visiting their home, Barbara started to tell me about Christianity. She was attending a missionary college and I was interested to know more. Her brother was annoyed by my interest, as he thought of his sister as a 'Bible-basher' and had absolutely no patience with what he referred to as her 'religious garbage'. She had enough sensitivity to realise that continuing to talk in front of him was only going to aggravate him and wouldn't be helpful to me, so we planned to meet privately the next afternoon and continue our discussion.

The following day she patiently answered my questions and went on to explain how I could become a Christian. Although I had been exposed to Christianity firstly at the Catholic kindergarten I had attended as a small child and then later at Sunday school, no one had explained Christianity to me in this way.

Barbara talked about sin[4], and the grace and forgiveness of God. She talked about Jesus Christ and what it meant to have a personal relationship with him. She talked about the Bible and how God spoke to us through his word. Everything she said made sense and was explained simply and clearly. I was touched very deeply, and I wanted what God was offering me that day. We prayed together, and I asked Jesus Christ to forgive me for my sins and to come into my life as my Saviour and Lord.

I bought myself my first Bible, and I started to attend the same local church as Barbara. I loved it. The people were caring, and I became particularly close to one wonderful old saint by the name of Monica Farrell.

Miss Farrell, as I called her, was a published author and did a great deal of public speaking. Of all the people in the church, she was my favourite.

I loved being with her. There was a distinct presence about her, which I – even as a young Christian – could recognise as the presence of Jesus. Sometimes she would ask me over for a meal and then we would have a Bible study together. These were precious times, but unfortunately for me, she did so much travelling and public speaking I was unable to spend as much time with her as I would have liked. She was, in fact, the only person who attempted to disciple me. Looking back now, I think what really blessed me the most was her total and unconditional acceptance of me. That sort of love and encouragement had a very powerful effect on me.

The other thing I loved about church was the worship. It was the time of one of the Billy Graham crusades in Sydney, and we sang many of the songs from the rallies. The songs were wonderful. In fact, everything was new and I couldn't get enough of it. I soaked up the teaching and always had questions to ask at every Bible study.

Someone in my church lent me Isobel Kuhn's autobiography *By Searching* to read. It was both encouraging and enlightening for me to see how God was with her in her journey. In time I bought and read all of her books. Her writing introduced me to the world of the missionary. As I read, I was transported to China – and in particular, Lisuland – where Isobel worked high in the mountains among the tribespeople. She described China and the lives and struggles of the people in such a way that both the country and the people became very real to me. She genuinely loved these people, and through the stories of their spiritual journeys I learned to love them as well. However, the most important thing about Isobel Kuhn's books for me was her honesty. She struggled, and she was honest about it. It was so encouraging to be exposed to someone who was real about their walk with God and was honest enough to document it.

This was a time of growth and discovery. There was so much to find out about God, and I was enjoying every minute of it. I was very committed and very happy.

The sexual attraction I felt towards men was still there, but as I didn't know what to do about it, I did nothing.

One Sunday the minister introduced a group of us to Richard, who had just come to our church from another state. In time the deep desire for sexual union with another man outweighed my desire for God, and I exchanged my allegiance to God for a sexual relationship with Richard.

CHAPTER 3

Disillusionment Bears Fruit

'This is what the Lord says:
Cursed are those who put their trust in mere humans,
who rely on human strength and turn their hearts away from the Lord.
They are like stunted shrubs in the desert, with no hope for the future.
They will live in the barren wilderness, in an uninhabited salty land.
But blessed are those who trust in the Lord and have made the Lord their hope and confidence.
They are like trees planted along a riverbank, with roots that reach deep into the water.
Such trees are not bothered by the heat or worried by long months of drought.
Their leaves stay green, and they never stop producing fruit.'

Jeremiah 17:5–8

My prayer had been, 'God, just give me one more chance at a relationship, and if it doesn't work out this time, I'll come back to you.' It wasn't long after I prayed this prayer that I met Alex.

The relationship started out as many gay relationships do. This was it, the one we had both been waiting for. But it wasn't very long before this relationship proved to be one of the worst experiences of the entire time I had spent living as a homosexual. If I needed an experience like this to sicken me completely of the homosexual scene, this was certainly it.

Two broken people do not make a healthy relationship. There were faults on both sides, and we were both using one another in different ways. I used Alex to try and fill the emotional neediness within me. Alex used me in other ways, including financially. It wasn't long before the relationship became blatantly manipulative, and from there it became very hurtful and bitter for both of us. When it finally ended, I felt completely drained and even more disillusioned with homosexuality and everything that went with it.

Looking back, I can see that God had answered my prayer by letting me go into this relationship, as I was now very seriously questioning my involvement with homosexuality.

None of the relationships I had been in had worked. In fact, as I thought about it, each of them had been emotionally damaging in some way. I was now finally beginning to question much of the gay propaganda I had believed, instead of just accepting it. One of the popular beliefs in the gay culture was that of the faithful, long-term relationship. It was portrayed as being exactly the same as heterosexual marriage except it was with a person of the same sex. But where were these faithful and happy relationships? I certainly hadn't experienced any, and I was becoming increasingly disillusioned with the promiscuity that, in my experience, was an integral part of the homosexual community.

After the disastrous relationship with Alex ended, I began to look very closely at many of the people I knew. I began to recognise how seriously damaged most of them were – and if they were damaged, what about me? I was also very conscious of the high abuse of drugs and alcohol in the scene, and I was abusing both of these substances myself. I had begun to use marijuana on a regular basis to deaden the loneliness I felt. It was fast becoming a psychologically addictive drug for me, and I was aware that I was using it to escape from my life. I still believed that homosexuality was not morally right for me. I had never lost my awareness of God, and deep down I knew the day was fast approaching when I was going to have to sort out my relationship with him.

One Saturday afternoon, I had a very soul-searching conversation with a friend. We started by confiding to each other about our dissatisfaction with our lives. One of the things we had both believed for many years was that our lives would be different if we could just find that 'special person'. This led to a discussion of the people we knew who were together as couples.

Although we had each spent about fifteen years as active homosexuals, we couldn't think of *any* couple we knew who was in a faithful relationship. In fact, we could think of very few – including ourselves – who were even *happy*.

The couples we knew had sex with others as well as their partners. Often the partners knew about the infidelity, but sometimes they didn't. Some of these couples had group sex or anonymous sex in public toilets or bathhouses. *We knew no one who was in a faithful relationship*. Many were also either drinking heavily or using drugs on a regular basis, and in some cases they were doing both. We all seemed to be on a merry-go-round of alcohol, drugs and promiscuous sex, waiting for Mr Wonderful to come along and rescue us by transforming our lives with instant fulfilment. I came to the conclusion that afternoon that between us we had spent thirty years chasing something that just did not exist.

I was beginning to recognise and face reality. However, acknowledging and accepting the truth was painful – it meant that I would have to let go of what I had believed, and also what I had hoped for, up until then.

I wondered if it could be any different elsewhere, so I decided to go to America. I took three months leave from my job, and off I went to see if that illusive relationship might be waiting for me overseas.

When I think back on that trip, my memories are a mixture of sight-seeing; shopping; gay bars and discos with names such as 'Toad Hall', 'Oil Can Harry's', and 'Busby's'; as well as brilliant stage shows and musicals.

One show that stands out in particular was *The Wiz*, which was an all-black musical version of *The Wizard of Oz*. It was a wonderful show, but a large part of the pleasure for me was the audience. It was mostly black, and I had never been part of a group of people where there was such a lack of inhibition. They were totally engaged from the overture until the last song. They clapped and swayed, and their reaction to what was happening on stage made it impossible not to be infected by their sheer exuberance. I can remember seeing the same musical in Sydney some time later, and it was quite flat compared with the New York version.

America was all new to me and a novelty to start with. In time though, I quickly discovered that the homosexual culture in Honolulu, San Francisco, Los Angeles, Boston and New York was really not so different from that of Sydney. There was certainly more of it and in many ways it was more blatant, but it didn't take long before I recognised that the same promiscuity bred the same desperation, loneliness and emptiness as it did back home. And of course, I didn't meet the perfect partner.

When I returned home, I knew I needed to do some very serious thinking. I had been actively involved in homosexuality for fifteen years.

That was a long time to come to the realization that it didn't work. Nor had I seen it work for anyone I knew. I couldn't believe I had been involved in it for so long. The time had gone so quickly, and there was nothing to show for it. The lifetime relationship I spent years looking for hadn't materialised.

Most of the focus amongst male homosexuals is on youth. If one is young and good-looking, one is much more likely to be accepted, have an easy time meeting sexual partners, and overall be more popular. In general, they will fit into the homosexual community more easily. It is all very shallow and superficial. In the places where I socialised the most, one never saw the much older men. There was only one bar I was aware of where the clientele was more mature, and we used to call it, quite cruelly, 'The Senior Citizen's Club'. So the prospect of growing old and alone in the homosexual world was something which filled me with dread. I saw the contempt with which older gays were treated and spoken about, and that wasn't something I was going to put myself through.

I knew I needed to make some very serious decisions about my life. I didn't know what sort of life God might have for me, but I reasoned that what ever it might involve, I couldn't be worse off than I already was. I may well have to remain celibate for the rest of my life, but at least I would be doing it with God.

I acknowledged to myself that I had had enough. I sat down and prayed. It wasn't a dramatic prayer, just a sincere repentance for the sin I was responsible for and the years I had wasted. After praying in that way, I rededicated my life to him.

I had finally come out. The date was September 4, 1976.

Many years have passed now, and although I have had ups and downs, I have never regretted my choice to leave homosexuality and to come back to God.

CHAPTER 4

The Journey Resumed

'It is God's truth that one loving spirit sets others on fire.'

Amy Carmichael, *Gold Cord*[5]

I wish I could say that once I left the homosexual community and recommitted myself to God, I lived happily ever after, but it wasn't like that at all for me.

I really felt that I had entered another world, and it was a world that felt upside down to begin with.

Previously I had been a 'night' person, but now I found myself at home and in bed – alone – quite early. Another thing that changed was the way I spent Sunday. It used to be a day which was usually depressing, and I mostly spent it recovering from the heavy drinking and drugs of Saturday night. Now it felt different. The drug and alcohol hangovers were gone, as was the depression.

One of the first things I did was to start having a regular time of prayer and Bible study each day with God, as I had done years before. I very quickly realised that this wouldn't just *happen*; I needed to be disciplined and to set a time aside for this. This became a time I looked forward to. I had no problem connecting to God. I read my Bible, prayed, and sometimes just sat quietly and enjoyed the peace of my apartment.

This quietness felt strange at first, yet after a while I realised that I was playing music less and was content just to sit and to enjoy the silence. It was a revelation to realise how much noise I continually surrounded myself with, and I wondered if I had done this to stop myself thinking. It was as if I had created a 'soundtrack' to my life. I had loads of recordings, many of which were vocal recordings. The particular type of music I remember playing a lot was what I have come to call 'loser' music. These were usually sad 'victim-type' songs. Imagine constantly filling your head with that sort of thing. It's no wonder I had viewed life so negatively and felt miserable a lot of the time.

I also gradually began to feel a deep, peaceful sense of security. I was aware that this was coming from my relationship with God. I felt *safe*, and it was a strange and new feeling for me. I no longer felt I needed to strive, because whatever the future held for me it was *his* future – a future that was now in his hands, no longer in mine. The constant hunger for someone to fill the vacuum and ease the loneliness, and the constant searching that went with it, had stopped.

As time went by I realised more and more that if left to my own desires and inclinations, things just did not work. When I left God out of my life everything went destructively wrong. The Bible tells us this, but I found it out the hard way – by painful experience. I hoped that I would never have to learn this lesson again.

One day, during one of these devotional times with God, I was reading Psalm 32. As I came to verse 8 the words leapt off the page at me: 'I will instruct you and teach you the way you should go; I will counsel you with my eye upon you' (RSV). I felt that God was giving this promise to me personally. This was incredibly reassuring, because I was able to admit to myself how foolish my past choices had been. It was a comfort now to realise that God was going to show me *how* to walk the journey I had resumed with him. I also felt that the verse was a lifetime promise for me.

I quickly realised the need to become involved in a church, so I started attending a small congregation in the suburb where I lived. I now looked forward to going to church and having the company of the new people I was beginning to get to know. Although it was tiny and only had a membership of about twenty or so people – and that was on a day when everyone turned up – it seemed to be exactly what I needed, as there was an intimacy there which I may not have found in a larger church.

As the months went by I realised some of my attitudes were changing. When I was a part of the homosexual community, my thinking about 'straight' society had been contemptuous at best. I suppose, in some ways, I saw 'straights' as 'the enemy'. This probably had a great deal to do with my perception of society's view of homosexuality. But as I got to know the people in my church, I gradually felt my respect for them growing.

I wouldn't have thought this was possible earlier, but the values I had despised I was now beginning to esteem.

There was one particularly hospitable family in the congregation, and most Sundays they would invite a group of us to spend the day with them. This was a time I grew to love, as it provided friendship as well as a lot of enjoyment and pleasure. A typical Sunday would be attending church in the morning and then going on to have lunch with this family. We would sit around and talk the afternoon away, and after a small evening meal we would end up back at church that night for the evening service. As well as being with people whom I really enjoyed, they gave me a very healthy family model – one which I had not experienced growing up.

The rest of the week was a different matter. It was lonely, as much of my time was spent on my own. There were times when I missed parts of my past life and some of the friends I had left, but as I felt unable to share these feelings with anyone, my past remained closed and was something I never spoke about at church.

In leaving homosexuality, I had left an entire community with its own culture. For example, it had its own dress codes, vocabulary, music, entertainers, humour and morality. I went into a community – the church – with its own culture, dress code, vocabulary, music and moral code. Whilst I had absolutely no regrets about my decision to come out, I missed many aspects of my former life, and the new life demanded a great deal of change on my part.

Everything was different, and there were times when I was in culture shock. I had come from the hectic, fast-paced and at times bizarre homosexual culture, into the radically different atmosphere of the church.

Getting used to the way people expressed themselves was at times strange. There were times when I felt we were speaking a different language. In fact, sometimes we were, as some of the older members of the congregation spoke to God in Elizabethan English!

I also had to adjust to the very quaint ways some people prayed. One day, a dear old saint prayed for a couple who were going on holidays. He asked God to bless this couple with 'journeying mercies' for the trip they were about to take. I wondered what on earth 'journeying mercies' could possibly be. The only thing I could think of was clean toilets on the way to where they were going.

Humour has always been important to me, and I found I missed the 'camp' humour I had been used to. Many of the gays I knew were quick-witted, clever, and at times sharp and bitchy in their humour, and in many cases were often willing to laugh at themselves. I missed this, as I found very little humour at all in the church and people tended to take things very seriously. There were times when my sense of the ridiculous was at odds with this seriousness, and often I just kept quiet as I was fairly sure my comments and views would have been completely misunderstood.

These were small things, but there were other things I have never been able to adjust to. At times I was hurt by, and angry about the misconceptions about gays and the church's attitudes and beliefs about homosexuality. Although the small church I had joined didn't put homosexuals down in this way, the general attitude regarding homosexuality in the wider church seemed to be that it was a worse sin than any other, even though there was no scriptural evidence to support this. Gays were spoken of as if they were beyond redemption and not worth bothering about.

Many people equate the church's attitude to homosexuals with that of God's attitude to homosexuals. But the two couldn't be more different in my view. God loves all his creation and longs for us to come to him. I was fortunate in that I always saw church bigotry for what it was – ignorance. I loved some of the people I had mixed with from my past, and it was particularly hurtful to hear such blatant ignorance passing for Christian teaching. Years later it still amazes me when I see how so many Christians have incorporated their prejudices and their cultural attitudes into their Christian beliefs.

Celibacy was another adjustment I had to make. After being sexually active for over fifteen years, there were times when being celibate had its difficulties – as anyone who has broken off a sexual relationship, been widowed or divorced can perhaps relate to. Sometimes I just longed for touch. I have always been affectionate by nature, and now the lack of touch was very difficult; there were times when I just ached for it.

I never had a problem relating to women, but learning to relate to heterosexual men was something I struggled with, as it didn't come naturally to me. I had grown up surrounded by women. Firstly, there were the women in my family, and then the neighbours I was closest to had all been women. A woman led me to Christ, and it was a woman who discipled me. My favourite authors were also women. Now I found myself mixing with 'straight' men for the first time, and I had nothing in common with them. Many men could talk of nothing but sport, and that has always been something I have had no interest in. I found cricket and football as riveting as watching paint dry. Without being able to resort to sport as a subject, I really had to work very hard to have even a superficial conversation with 'the lads'.

I would have given anything for someone to talk with about what was happening to me, including the adjustments I was making. But I was not at a point where I felt I could trust anyone, given the attitudes I had picked up from Christians about homosexuals and homosexuality.

Although in many ways it was a lonely time, in other ways it was exciting. I knew God was with me, and I was on a journey of discovery both about God and about myself.

During this time, an old lady who lived in the apartment beneath me was admitted to hospital. One day, as I was getting ready to go to work, I felt God say, 'Go and visit Mrs Gray.' It wasn't an audible voice I heard – more like a very strong internal voice accompanied by the conviction that this was something I really should do.

However, visiting this old lady was the last thing I felt like doing. She drank heavily, and I suspected that she would in all probability want me to go and buy her alcohol. I wondered how I was going to say 'no' to that, if she should ask.

I tried to find an excuse for not going, but as I couldn't, I reluctantly went. At the last minute, on my way out the door, I took some flowers someone had given to me, and as a very last thought, I also took a couple of missionary biographies with me. The visit went well; I gave Mrs Gray the flowers and the books, and surprisingly didn't have a problem in saying 'no' to going to the pub for her. I went off to work wondering if I really had heard God, or if it had just been an overactive imagination. Anyway, I had done it and was relieved that the visit was over. I would just have to let God sort out my 'delusions'.

A couple of months later I was talking to one of the guys who lived in the same apartment block. He said, 'Did you know Mrs Gray died?'

'No, I didn't,' I replied, 'How did you know – did you visit her?'

'Yes, I saw her regularly, but she became quite peculiar towards the end. Someone had given her some books to read about a missionary, and they had a weird effect on her. She started to pray, asked for a Bible, and went all religious, really – it was quite strange.'

I like to think I *did* hear God that day.

I had no doubt I was in the right church. I was growing again as a Christian after my many years away from God. As well as the growth I was experiencing, I felt loved by the people in the church, and this was very affirming.

It was a church that practised adult baptism, and I was baptised shortly after I joined them. Being baptised changed something for me. The physical act of being immersed had a profound effect, and whilst I couldn't fully comprehend what happened spiritually, inwardly I was *different*. Much of the power of the old way of life had been broken, and my attitudes were different. The things which were important and attractive to me previously were now becoming less so, and my values generally were undergoing a change.

We also took communion each Sunday, and I knew this strengthened me. Once again, I couldn't understand the full implications of it; I just knew it really strengthened me spiritually and emotionally.

One other thing which was particularly helpful about this church was the strong sense of acceptance and belonging which was conveyed to me. I never felt I was a 'project'. When I was invited to something, I knew it was because I was wanted and not because someone felt sorry for me. To have felt I was someone's 'good deed' would have been both humiliating and degrading and would have undermined much of the healing God was doing at this time.

Time was passing very quickly, and as I looked back I could see many changes were taking place in my life.

I was firmly established in a church where I was happy and felt comfortable. I knew I was liked and valued by the people, and this was mutual, which was important to me. Although I was lonely at times, the friendships at church were becoming more established, and I was beginning to trust these people more and more. I knew I was still sexually attracted to men, but the desires were not nearly as powerful as they had been. I didn't know what to do about my same-sex attraction, so I did nothing. I wasn't aware of needing professional help, and if I had been I wouldn't have known where to get it anyway. I wanted intimacy with God, and that was what was happening.

I had read in Jeremiah 29:13 'You will seek me and find me; when you seek me with all your heart' (RSV). Now, I didn't know or care if I was taking this verse out of context. I just knew I wanted God with all my heart, and he said I would find him by searching for him. If changes were happening in me, then they were a by-product of this search. My primary goal was God; anything else that happened was a bonus. It was just God being God and revealing his incredible love, gentleness and kindness to me.

At this time, I knew of nothing that had been written for people who wanted to deal with unwanted same-sex attraction. Of course, material may have existed, but if it did I hadn't seen it. I didn't know what God had for me in the future, but as I looked back over the time that had passed since my exit from the homosexual community, I felt things were going very well.

When I came out of homosexuality, God took me into what I can only describe as like living in a desert. I felt isolated and, except for God, I was alone in that place. Apart from the friends in my church, there were very few people around. It was a time when I was so lonely that I went to God for the comfort I needed, as there was nowhere else to go. In looking back from the vantage point of time, I am very grateful to him for putting me in this place, as I wouldn't have known him to the degree I do now if I had not embraced such an experience and drawn what I needed directly from him. I also realise in looking back that it was a time when God was gently deepening my trust in him. In retrospect I now realise what a great deal of work he had to do in me. Some of that was going to be painful, and to go through that pain I needed to trust him and know he loved me. The 'desert time' helped me to do that.

All my life I have been blessed with a love of reading. As a child I used books as a means of escape. However, during my time in the 'desert', reading became not only a source of comfort but also a very effective way of learning some of the lessons God wanted to teach me.

The apostle Paul wrote that 'All Scripture is inspired by God and is useful to teach us what is true and to make us realise what is wrong in our lives. It corrects us when we are wrong and teaches us to do what is right. God uses it to prepare and equip his people to do every good work' (2 Timothy 3:16,17). I have never had a problem in believing that the Bible was inspired by God. If this is so, it follows that it is completely trustworthy. The belief of the divine inspiration of the Bible has been widely held by the church throughout the ages.

Christianity is a revealed faith, in the sense that Jesus Christ is God's revelation to us of himself. We are told that 'The Son radiates God's own glory and expresses the very character of God' (Hebrews 1:3a). God has shown us his character and his great love for us through the life of his Son.

The way we learn about Jesus is through what is recorded about him in the Bible. Therefore, when I came back to God, my primary focus was the Bible. I spent hours reading and praying through this incredible book. I was also aware of the need to apply what I was reading to my life. It was all very well to study, pray and have an intellectual understanding of what the Bible contained, but if it didn't bring me closer to God what was the point? I wasn't reading the Bible to polish my theology; I was reading it to know God. And as I wanted to know the author personally, I read with the aim of meeting God in an intimate way. I learned to love and respect God through the Bible, and I learned to draw from him the comfort, strength and the direction I needed.

As I read the Bible and put into place the principles contained there, God slowly but surely revealed himself to me. I became increasingly aware of his personal interest in me and my welfare, and I learned more about his patience and his compassion. I gradually began to appreciate more fully the incredible gift of Jesus Christ and all that he had achieved for us by his death. The Gospel of John was a particular favourite of mine, with its intimate and touching portrait of Jesus. I saw God through the life of Jesus. As I read, I grew in my trust of God, and as I grew in this trust, I was able to open myself more to him.

I remember, after I had completed reading through the whole of the Old Testament for the first time, how stunned I was to realise just how much I had behaved like the Israelites. My nature contained the same rebellion, selfishness and stubborn stupidity. Yet God was showing me such gentle patience. I kept asking myself – and him – why he even bothered. My daily time with God was something I valued and looked forward to. It was not a duty or a religious ritual to be performed. Rather, it was a privilege and a time of ever-deepening intimacy with him that I still look forward to.

As well as the Bible, I read Christian books. This was the best way for me to tap into the wisdom and experience of others. In particular, I loved the biographies and autobiographies of Christians. I learned from their stories and the way God led them, and I learned from the way they had grown and lived their lives. I read everything helpful I could lay my hands on, but one of the most helpful authors – and the one I loved the most – was Amy Carmichael.

As I have already said, when I first became a Christian, Isobel Kuhn's books were a big influence. She quoted Amy Carmichael so often, that one day I decided to investigate this woman's writings for myself. I am glad I did, because my spiritual journey would have been very much poorer without the influence of this beautiful lady.

Amy Beatrice Carmichael was born in 1867, in Northern Ireland. She served for a short while as a missionary in Japan until she became sick and returned home. When she recovered her health she set out again and went to South India as a missionary, where she remained until her death in 1951.

The work she founded was called the Dohnavur Fellowship, and it focussed on saving children who would have been sold to the temples to eventually become temple prostitutes. She created a family where these children were raised in an atmosphere of love and Christian values, and the work continues to this day.

There are excellent biographies about Amy Carmichael and the work she did. However, the books that influenced me most in those early days were the books she wrote herself. It may seem strange to some that a woman who began her life in the Victorian era should have had such an influence for good in the life of someone who had left homosexuality, but that's the way it was.

Some Christians are fortunate to have mentors. The Macquarie Dictionary gives the meaning of the word mentor as 'a wise and trusted adviser'. I never had that sort of relationship. If I had, I may have become overly dependent on them, and could have ended up relying on them instead of God for my spiritual nurture. But in those very crucial early years, God gave me a very precious gift in giving me the books of Amy Carmichael.

What was so great about this missionary whom I never met and who died when I was eight years old? Well, as I read about her life, and in particular the way she really knew God and related to him, she provided me with a Christian model which I had never known. It was through her books that I learnt more about God's incredible love for us. *Her* relationship with her heavenly Father gave me a glimpse of what *my* relationship with him could be. She had a passion for God, for Jesus, and for broken people that has been a lasting influence in my life.

Amy wrote from her own experience of God, and what she wrote impacted my life in such a way that I will always be grateful for this woman and the way God used her. As she opened up to me more fully the nature of God, she showed me that this was a God whom I could trust.

She wrote about his provision for the Dohnavur family, and as I saw the way in which he provided for them, I realised he would also provide for me. She taught me about how God was with her in her difficulties and pain, and I realised that he was with me in mine. But the most important thing I discovered from her books was the tenderness and kindness of God, and the very great depth of his love for his children. God's love came through to me from these books, especially his father love, and that was something I particularly needed to know. I had immersed myself in the gay culture because I was looking for love, but now I was being shown the *real* thing. It is no wonder I read and re-read Amy Carmichael's books; they were the closest I had come to seeing this *authentic* love in action.

She was also an extremely practical person. Take, for example, her three suggestions for prayer:

1. We don't need to explain to our Father things that are known to Him.
2. We don't need to press Him, as if we had to deal with an unwilling God.
3. We don't need to suggest to Him what to do, for He himself knows what to do.[6]

I still find these suggestions for prayer helpful.

Did I idolise her? I don't believe I did. She pointed me to God, and I think he used her life and her books to reveal himself more clearly to me.

Amy Carmichael was a bit like what I imagine a spiritual mother to be. In fact, I'd go as far as to say that apart from my wife Truda, she has probably influenced me more than any other person.

Those of us who have not had a healthy image of God as a father need to correct our distorted images of him. The way I have been helped to do this has been through God's revelation of himself in the Bible. I have also been helped through others of God's children, who have walked with him and known him intimately, and were willing to pass on their experiences of him to others.

I am always conscious of how people who choose not to read for various reasons disadvantage themselves by not availing themselves of the riches of the Bible, as well as the wealth of the good Christian literature that is available.

Although I wasn't aware of it at the time, what I was going through was a process of feeding and starving. I was feeding myself by reading the Bible and good Christian books, spending time in fellowship with other Christians, and listening to the teaching at church. I was starving myself of the old habits and practices I had been involved in for so many years by not going to bars and clubs, not sleeping with men, and in general – trying as best I could – to leave the old life and habits and move on into the new.

It would have been wonderful if a magic wand had been waved and I could have been instantly transformed into a healthy heterosexual male with no problems. But to expect that sort of 'Walt Disney' magic was not only unrealistic, it was impossible. After all, God doesn't obliterate our past.

It would also have been nice if my journey had been smooth and consistent, but it wasn't. There were times when I moved forward and there were times – many of them – when I felt I was going backwards.

I knew God was with me, but there were times when I would have loved to have been really open with other people about the struggle. Even though I was reading, praying and attending church regularly, I was still lonely at times. There were also times when I was tempted to go back to the familiarity of the homosexual world – not for the sex, but just to be with people with whom I had things in common. I had no idea if what I was experiencing would ever end or improve, or if the pain and loneliness I was feeling would ever decrease. Some days I just held on to God by what seemed to be a very fine thread.

Someone once said that where there is building there is a lot of rubbish.

I knew God was building something, but there was such a lot of rubbish in my life that sometimes the rubbish was all I could see. It was a day-to-day struggle, and I wouldn't be honest if I didn't admit that some days I felt like giving up entirely. The times of discouragement and loneliness were made harder than they needed to be, by my perceived attitude of what the people in my church would think if I came out and talked about my homosexuality. My sense of isolation magnified my problems enormously.

Forgiveness was something God was teaching me at this time. Gradually I became aware that I needed to forgive my father for what he had not given me. In my head I told myself Dad had done his best for me, but in my heart I was still hurting just like a small child because he had never shown me any interest or affection. I always felt he was disappointed with me and had never particularly liked me. This may or may not have been the truth, but it was my perception. All my life I told myself it didn't matter. I was an adult, and many people had much worse childhoods than I had, but telling myself this did not diminish the pain. It just sent it down to a place deep inside me, where it lay dormant and undealt with. Now the time had come to do something about it, and the first step I needed to take was forgiveness. Even though my Dad had been dead for years and I was unsure of the theology of extending forgiveness to a dead person, it was the only step I could see that was going to be a help to me. So I forgave him.

None of this happened instantaneously. It took time for the awareness to dawn. Over a period of time I prayed and thanked God for the good in my father. I went on to acknowledge the areas where he had not provided me with what I needed or wanted. He should have intervened and protected me when my uncle abused me but hadn't, so I forgave him for that. He should have been a better role model but couldn't, so I forgave him for that. I would have liked him to have shown me physical affection, but he didn't – either through choice or incapability – so I forgave him for that too. I went through everything I could think of, and when I finished praying I asked God to accept my forgiveness and I released my father from whatever I had been holding against him. I also let go to God any of my unmet needs and expectations. I told God that he would have to be the father I had never had and provide me with all the things I had missed out on.

This transaction was as honest as I could make it and I can't really say I felt very different afterwards – but I had done it.

Later when I read Leanne Payne's book *The Healing of the Homosexual*, I understood the need for forgiveness much better. She says:

> In cases of homosexuality, the rejection of a parent often needs to be confessed and renounced before the person can find wholeness. I find this to be the case time and again in both men and women. For a young lad to seriously reject his own father (even with 'good reason') is often to find that, as an adult, he has rejected his own masculinity. He has rejected, in a manner of speaking, his father within himself. Through prayer, the son can be helped to accept his father, while at the same time he can reject and repudiate any of his father's sinful actions. In cases where the father has been particularly ignoble, hostile, or brutal, the son has difficulty in separating the sin from the sinner, I lead him in a prayer of thanksgiving to God for all he created the parent to be. Then we go into prayer where forgiveness is extended to the father for not becoming that completed person in Christ. The way is paved for God to touch and heal the father within the son, including the genetic inheritance from his father with all its potential in the very cells of the son's being.[7]

I recognised this was my experience.

Years later I now realise my father has passed on to me some wonderful things. Some time after I forgave Dad, I was speaking with a relative who knew my father very well, much better than I ever had. She told me things about Dad's personality that I recognise as things that are in mine. I believe that because I have forgiven him, I have removed a block and I can now accept and embrace those parts of myself which I have inherited from him. Over time, I have been able to think of him with love, and I now realise that within his limitations, he really did do the best he was capable of for his family.

To be able to get to that place I needed to deal with my feelings in an honest way. I did not pretend I hadn't suffered, or that his inability to love me in ways I could recognise and relate to hadn't affected my life, because it had. I also did not diminish or trivialise the result of not being able to enter into a loving relationship with him. It had an effect on me, and I was able to admit that and grieve the lack of it.

After forgiving my father, I went on to forgive the other people whom I felt had hurt me in some way. It took time to do this. It needed to be genuine and not superficial. I forgave the uncle who interfered with me as a child. I forgave the other uncle who had exposed himself to me. I forgave the kids who called me names as I was growing up. I forgave my previous lovers of anything which I felt needed my forgiveness. I also forgave myself for making so many wrong and stupid choices in my life. I made it as thorough as I could, and as people came to mind that I felt needed my forgiveness, I cleaned the slate and brought each of them before God.

How we need to take forgiveness seriously. And what freedom forgiveness brings. Many years after all of this took place, Truda and I were asked to pray with an old lady who had a very bad knee and who was having trouble being able to walk up the stairs to her apartment. We prayed for her, but nothing much seemed to happen. After waiting a while in silence, Truda asked her if there was anybody she felt she needed to forgive. She was thoughtful for a time and then told us about a friendship she had many years previously which ended in a lot of bitterness after an argument. She talked about it for a while, expressed some of the feelings, and after some time Truda gently asked her if she could find it in her heart to forgive her friend for what she had done. The old lady thought about it and then said she felt she could do it if we could help her find the right words to say to God. We led her in a prayer of forgiveness and then encouraged her to ask God to bless the friend wherever she was. The next week the old lady practically *skipped* up to us. We could barely believe our eyes, as she had hardly been able to walk the week before. She told us she met her friend *that very week* for the first time in many years. She was able to tell her she had no bad feelings towards her any more. Not only that, but she was now able to walk without any difficulty at all.

Who knows what blessings we miss out on by not being obedient to Jesus' commandment to forgive others the way we want God to forgive us?[8] I believe the strong feelings that are often involved when someone wounds us – for example, hurt, anger, hatred and sometimes the desire for revenge – need also to be acknowledged and brought to God. Some Christians may be afraid, as I was, to even be able to admit we have such feelings. But it is good to realise God will not disown us if we bring our feelings to him. I love the honesty of the writers of the Psalms and take comfort from the fact that others have gone before me and given us their example.

CHAPTER 5

Sometimes It Hurts

'What is REAL?' asked the Rabbit one day, when they were lying side by side near the nursery fender, before Nana came to tidy the room. 'Does it mean having things that buzz inside you and a stick-out handle?'
'Real isn't how you are made,' said the Skin Horse. 'It's a thing that happens to you. When a child loves you for a long, long time, not just to play with, but REALLY loves you, then you become Real.'
'Does it hurt?' asked the Rabbit.
'Sometimes,' said the Skin Horse, for he was always truthful. 'When you are Real you don't mind being hurt.'
'Does it happen all at once, like being wound up,' he asked, 'or bit by bit?'
'It doesn't happen all at once,' said the Skin Horse. 'You become. It takes a long time. That's why it doesn't often happen to people who break easily, or have sharp edges, or who have to be carefully kept. Generally, by the time you are Real, most of your hair has been loved off, and your eyes drop out and you get loose in the joints and very shabby. But these things don't matter at all, because once you are Real you can't be ugly, except to people who don't understand.'
Margery Williams, *The Velveteen Rabbit*[9]

It was about a year or so after I had started attending my small church that I decided I would like a change one Sunday, so I decided to attend a service in another denomination. I sat there before the service began and for a while I just let the music wash over me, but I found my attention focussing on a young woman who was sitting in the row in front of me. I realised I was staring at this woman but was unable to stop. As I looked, I was aware of how beautiful she was. I was fascinated by her hair, her glowing skin, and her overall loveliness. I was aware of a purity about this young woman that I realised I had never seen in any of the homosexual men I knew. I was absolutely fascinated by her, and I slowly began to realise that there was a strong sexual component in my attraction. This came as a tremendous shock, and I sat there stunned for a while.

Over the next few months I wondered about the ramifications of what had happened to me in church that day. What had changed? Why was

I now less attracted sexually to men than I was previously? Why had I found myself being attracted to this woman, and where did the sexual part of the attraction come from? Was I capable of having a relationship with a woman? If so, would marriage be an option for me? Maybe I would not be on my own for the rest of my life. There were many other questions I asked myself as well.

As I thought about these things, it began to dawn on me that one of the assertions I accepted as 'truth' during my time in the gay community had now been seriously challenged.

I was told people who were homosexuals were born that way. 'Once gay, always gay, you're born that way.' I heard that so many times I just accepted it as a fact and incorporated it into my belief system. But if that was true, why was I now much less attracted to men than I had been? What about the attraction to the young woman in church? That incident had shown me that my sexuality was far from fixed.

I had no answers at that time, and as far as I knew there were no books that would give me the answers to the questions I was asking myself. I didn't feel able to talk these sorts of things through with anyone, as there was still a great deal of shame attached to the subject of homosexuality for me. Even if I had felt courageous enough to speak with someone, to whom would I have gone? Overall, Christians seemed to be repelled by the whole subject of homosexuality. Being able to talk about some of the stuff I was thinking through, both objectively and without bigotry surfacing and taking over, didn't seem to be an option. And even if I had spoken about it, would they know any more than I did?

The shame I felt about my past was keeping me locked in silence. Years later, I realised the importance of good, healthy friendships where problems could be shared. However, at that time there was no one I would have talked these things through with, and I felt very vulnerable.

Even so, I felt I had experienced considerable change since my departure from the homosexual community about a year before. I felt more contented and was living a life that was vastly more rewarding and a whole lot less damaging than it had been when I was involved in homosexuality. I thought about the many people I had known who drank heavily, as well as the ones who were involved with drugs. Gay! That word was another lie! I hadn't found it 'gay' in the original sense of the word. In my experience it was damaging, both for many of the people I knew as well as for myself. The 'glamour' of the homosexual world had, over time, proved to be a deception and a lie.

My job in staff training gave me opportunities to meet many people, and as the training classes usually lasted for about six weeks I got to know them really well. In one of these classes there was a young woman with whom I became very friendly.

Liz was good company, fun to be with, and also a Christian. We began having coffee after work and sometimes she would drive me home. These times became very precious to me as Liz was an excellent listener, and over time I found myself telling her more and more about myself. I shared with her about my childhood, my time in the gay community, my decision to leave it, and the isolation and struggle that had been involved in that journey. It was the first time I ever felt the freedom of unburdening, and it was a relief to empty myself and talk about these things with someone who knew how to listen and who accepted me unconditionally and without judgement.

Liz's family entertained a lot, and this was very different from my own family, where we were never able to ask friends home. I began to spend more and more time with Liz, as well as her family, and stayed at their home most weekends. I felt accepted, loved and very much one of the family.

In the warmth of my new-found acceptance by Liz and her family, my times with God diminished. In the excitement of all of this new 'family' relating, I stupidly must have thought I needed God less. As time went by, Liz and I began sleeping together. This also obviously contributed to my feeling distant from God, but I told myself 'not to worry' as we would in all likelihood marry.

And marry we did, but we ran into problems almost immediately. There were difficulties sexually. Even though we had slept together before we married, Liz now didn't want sex at all. I thought this was entirely my fault, even though I didn't know why. We didn't seem to be able to talk about it, as it was all too painful. Outwardly we pretended that everything was fine, but in reality that was far from the truth.

About six months after our marriage, Liz's sister was killed in an accident. This tragedy plunged us all into shock. I couldn't begin to understand the grief involved for Liz. She said it was as if part of her had died with her sister. She also said she wished she had died instead of her. I suppose her sister's death and our marriage problems, as well as not seeing any resolution, combined to bring about her despair.

We went for counselling but still did not find any real answers. One counsellor told Liz that he thought she had married me because she wanted to rescue me. Of course, I felt like the failure of all time and blamed myself for everything. Although my relationship with God was still intact, I felt hopeless and despaired of anything ever working out.

In time we separated. Liz moved back home and in my passivity, I waited for her to make up her mind about what we were going to do with the rest of our lives.

Shortly after we were married I had sold my apartment, and we had moved into a large house which I hated. I missed my old apartment even more than ever as I found myself in this house alone.

It was at this time I decided to go and talk to a counsellor. I wanted a Christian counsellor, so I decided to see someone at a Christian organisation offering face-to-face counselling. I poured out my story: my homosexuality, leaving that lifestyle, a broken marriage, and the despair I was now feeling. I assumed that the session was for an hour, but I was aware that it had gone on for much longer than that. I asked the counsellor about this and she replied, 'Oh, it's alright, I have to have supervision later and this will be a fascinating story to tell my supervisor.' I felt as though I had been punched in the stomach. I can remember walking away from her office feeling like an absolute freak. It was a very long time before I felt confident enough to trust another counsellor.

To say I felt a failure would be an understatement. The homosexual life and the relationships I had been involved in hadn't worked, and now this Christian marriage had failed. Perhaps I was just too emotionally crippled for any relationship? I dropped out of church, and apart from a couple of close friends I kept little contact with anyone.

Many years later, with a lot more understanding, I now realise that I was stuck in the grief process. I firmly believed that if I just waited long enough, the marriage would get back on track and everything would be alright. The separation went on for about two and a half years until we finally decided to end our mutual misery and divorced.

What went wrong?

Over the next few years I thought about the mistakes I had made. There were many. Firstly, I had been out of homosexuality only eighteen months when I married. The healing process had a long way to go before I would be ready for such a huge step as marriage. Secondly, we should never have become involved sexually. God is very specific about sex before marriage in his word. It was sin, and all sin has consequences. Thirdly, there was a lot of acceptance from both Liz and her family. That in itself had a powerful influence on me, as I was lonely and wanted to be a part of something I had never experienced before. Fourthly, an old pattern had re-emerged. As soon as someone came along and I became involved with them emotionally, I switched my affections from God to them and looked to them to meet my needs. It was the same thing I had done with Richard many years before. Fifthly, I had no concept of God's timing in my healing process. I thought that because I was attracted to Liz sexually, and was able to enjoyably engage in heterosexual sex, I was ready for marriage. What a costly, painful, and extremely damaging mistake my immaturity and disobedience had caused.

Perhaps if I had been willing to be open with others about my life, I wouldn't have found being listened to and accepted by Liz to be as powerful as it was. Perhaps if I had waited longer before rushing into this relationship, I would have had more perspective. Perhaps if we had not slept together, it would have been easier to back off before we were both so badly hurt.

I sold the house, and after the mortgage was paid, bought a very small apartment with what money was left and tried to get on with my life.

At that time I was friendly with a couple of gay men I worked with. I began to socialise with them by going out to dinner, movies and various places. Both men were in relationships with other men, and neither was sexually attractive to me. The company these guys and their partners offered, as well as their acceptance of me, broke some of the isolation I was living in.

As I revisited some of the gay restaurants and bars I used to frequent, I saw that nothing had changed since I left the community. It was the same atmosphere of desperation accompanied by the same emptiness. Whilst going back to this type of life permanently was not a consideration for me, I wondered if the future held anything for me as a Christian.

I now felt alien to both the gay community and the church. After all, wasn't divorce the unforgivable sin? Add to divorce my past homosexuality and I couldn't see a great deal of acceptance in the church for me. Or, I thought to myself, there would only be acceptance if I were silent about my past. As I thought about it, I realised I didn't miss the church at all really, but I did miss God.

It took time, but gradually my relationship with God became all it had been before. Although I avoided church, I was hungry to learn and I wanted to grow, so during the next couple of years I attended several self-development groups in my desire to grow and to work through my mess. I found these groups interesting, stimulating and extremely helpful. I gradually worked through a great deal to do with the marriage break-up, as well as many other things. These included my passivity and my lack of assertiveness. I loved the valuable insights these groups gave and enjoyed the people I met.

I also realised that not all of my problems were to do with the issue of homosexuality. There were people I met in these groups who struggled with some of the same things I did, but they did not come from a homosexual background.

I was involved in a process that was enabling me to grow in confidence.

Being able to understand both myself and others at a deeper level brought a great deal of freedom. I was learning listening skills, as well as how to communicate and express myself more clearly and appropriately. In this process, my passivity and lack of assertiveness were diminishing, and this led to my being able to initiate and develop new friendships.

I was also finding myself more at ease in the company of heterosexual men. Much of the fear and uneasiness I had felt in the presence of 'straight' men was decreasing, and I was becoming aware that these men were in fact just ordinary people. The mystery which had surrounded heterosexual men was diminishing, and I was beginning to feel more comfortable and relaxed in their company. The confidence I was gaining in my relating and communicating was helping me to feel good about myself, and as I felt better about myself, I was more able to reach out to others. This in turn broke the isolation I had lived in for most of my life.

The disastrous experience of this marriage break-up forced me to work on things which had certainly needed attention for a very long time. It also forced me to once again evaluate and choose the direction I wanted my life to take.

In time, I eventually came to realise that divorce was not the 'unforgivable sin' any more than homosexuality was. As lonely as my journey away from homosexuality turned out to be, and as painful and damaging as the break-up of my marriage was, I had grown through it. I was now a stronger person. I was also resolved in my decision not to go back to active homosexuality.

I had to admit that the journey had been made more difficult at times than it needed to have been by some of the choices I had made. I also knew it was a very slow process. I would have loved a quick, painless 'fix', but that just wasn't how it was.

CHAPTER 6

Climb or Die

'So if the Son sets you free, you are truly free.'
John 8:36

The question I am often asked is, 'How is a homosexual healed?'

However, I wonder if the question – or at least the thinking behind it – is flawed. It implies that if the person can find the right key – read the right book, talk to the right person, attend the right seminar, pray the right prayer, or be delivered of a demon – they will be instantly healed. Some people think that if God removes the unwanted 'homosexual bit' and replaces it with the much-wanted 'heterosexual bit', all will be well, and the person will then live happily ever after. But recovery from homosexuality is not as simple as changing a spark plug or a light globe.

I didn't pursue God specifically for change or recovery. I wouldn't have considered a change in my sexuality to be even a remote possibility; in fact, the thought would never have even entered my head. The changes in my character, as well as my sexuality, were changes God made in me over time as my relationship with him deepened.

I sought God for *himself*, and change was something that came out of that relationship. This wasn't change in *one* particular thing; it was change in *many* things. It was a process, and of course, processes take time – sometimes a long time. In the beginning I was totally unaware of how much of my life was going to be touched and transformed by God.

The first step in this process was deciding that I had had enough of homosexuality. I needed to make this choice for myself; no one could make it for me. My decision was made when I reached the point in my life where I was certain I had had enough of living a lifestyle that didn't work, was extremely damaging and brought neither fulfilment nor happiness.

The next step for me was inviting God back into my life. In time, I gave him permission to do whatever he wanted or needed to do in me, and I made a determined decision to accept whatever he had in store for me. As I did this, I was still unaware that changes were going to take place. I was just giving God permission to take charge after being in charge myself for so long. Much later, as I read about the process of recovery, I realised how important was the 'determined decision' I had made. I believe that by giving God that permission, it enabled him to do what he wanted to do in me. He doesn't violate us; he waits for an invitation to work in us.

Years later, I read a description of this strong determination by Gerard van den Aardweg, a Dutch psychologist. He describes it as a 'good will', saying:

> Without a strong determination, a 'good will', no change is possible. With it, improvement is certain in the majority of cases, and in a minority, even a cure – a deep inner change in overall neurotic emotionality and a beneficial reversal of sexual interests – is achievable.[10]

He continues:

> To persist in the resolution to change one must cultivate in oneself such motivators as a clear view of homosexuality as something unnatural; a sound moral and/or religious conviction; and, where applicable, the will to make the best of an existing marriage relationship that is reasonable, apart from the sexual aspect. Being well-motivated is not the same as practicing rigid self-bashing, self-hatred, or a fearful compliance with moral prescriptions simply because they are imposed by society or religion; rather, it is to have a quiet and strong feeling that homosexuality is incompatible with psychological maturity and/or moral purity, with the deepest stirrings of one's conscience, and with one's responsibility before God. To strengthen regularly one's moral resolution to fight the homosexual side of the personality is therefore crucial for a good outcome.[11]

One part of my recommitment to God involved my acknowledgement that I had been living in rebellion against him. I had deliberately chosen to live my life according to what I wanted. And surprise, surprise, it hadn't worked. So now I made another choice, which was to live my life by the guidelines God has given in his word, the Bible. This involved doing what the Bible said, even though at times it was the more difficult way.

I also needed to get to know God again, and that meant spending time with him by reading, praying, and understanding what he had already revealed to me about himself in the Bible.

Now, my intimate times with God were not just academic studies of the scriptures. I confided in him and I grieved with him. I sought – and found – intimacy with him. Of course, in doing this I was developing and deepening my relationship with him. And as this happened, I was able to trust him more.

St Augustine said: 'You made us for yourself, and our hearts are restless until they rest in You.'[12]

I have found that to be the truth. I didn't find rest and fulfilment by embracing a gay identity; I didn't find it in homosexual sex; I didn't find it in pursuing a career and making a lot of money, or owning my own home or any other thing the world said was important. I found that rest, fulfilment and healing in Jesus Christ.

I wasn't surprised when I read an article by Alan Medinger, a well-known author and respected ex-gay leader, who headed up a ministry to Christians in Baltimore for those struggling with unwanted homosexual feelings. In this article Medinger writes, 'Spend time with God. It is a radical thing to say, but I absolutely believe that the most important thing you can do to further your growth into manhood is to spend time with God.'[13]

Now some people may immediately react with 'I just don't have the time'. Those with this attitude will lose out. I can only say what worked for me. I made time. It was my priority, and I have held to it ever since those first days of leaving homosexuality all those years ago.

Self-discipline played a huge part here. Getting up early to spend time with God was at times difficult and not always convenient, but it was a priority. I knew what I could go back to, and that was no longer an option for me. I built in regularity, and that meant the less important things needed to go so I could spend this time each day with God. Praying in the shower or on the bus when I was on my way to work was not the same as a regular time kept to spend exclusively with God.

Gerard van den Aardweg comments on this:

> The next step is indispensable: *self-discipline*. For the most part, this concerns trivial things: waking up on time; keeping regular habits in taking care of one's body, in one's meals, clothing, hair; putting a reasonable order into the small affairs of everyday life and work, not delaying works or business that deserve priority; planning (roughly, not meticulously or obsessively) the day, one's amusement, social life. If there are points of shaky or absent self-discipline, note them and begin working on them. Many homosexually inclined people have difficulty with some form of self-discipline. To disregard these problems, hoping for an emotional cure that will solve everything else, is foolish. No (self-) therapy can satisfactorily succeed if this down-to-earth dimension of daily self-discipline is neglected. Invent simple methods for your characteristic weak spots. Start with one or two areas of failing self-discipline; when they improve, the rest will follow more easily.[14]

Self-discipline was the very thing that I never practiced in the way I had been living for fifteen years, so naturally it was something that took time and a great deal of effort to establish.

Having a practice of reading large quantities of the Bible was important for me. I wanted to understand and apply what I read, and this meant reading more than just one or two verses at odd times. It meant being systematic and disciplined in my approach to reading the scriptures. I still regularly read through the entire Bible and find that it gives me a balanced overview of the scriptures.

I was on a search for truth and direction. I found that direction in the Bible. In time, I came to see God as a Father who unconditionally loves *all* his children, regardless of their struggles. Through the scriptures, I realised that God cared about me and loved me. I learned healthy boundaries for living. It was from the scriptures that I learned the things

I needed to function as a whole person. While the Bible didn't 'cure' me, it gave me the grounding I needed as I continued to move forward in my recovery.

One of the dangers in telling a story like mine is that some people may be tempted to think that because they struggle with some of the same things I did – if they *do* what I did – they will end up with the same result. I have tried to share my journey honestly, but it is just that – *my* journey. Certainly there may be things that people can identify with, and there may be principles that will be relevant for others on *their* journey, but God treats all his children as individuals. My advice is not to look for a *pattern* to follow, but to follow *him*. He knows just what is important for each person. Trust him – he is trustworthy.

As I continued to move forward in my relationship with God, I realised that many things in my life were changing. The things I had valued and wanted previously were no longer important. Habits, values, beliefs and thinking patterns were undergoing changes.

In time, what I later came to recognise as the roots of my homosexuality were dealt with.

So what were the roots of my homosexuality? Although there may have been other factors, over many years I have been able to identify six things I believe contributed to my homosexuality. These were:

- the non-existent relationship with my father,
- the sexual assault I experienced as a child,
- the physical and emotional deprivation I felt in my family,
- the rejection I experienced from my peers growing up,
- the name-calling, or external labelling, and
- my own sinful choices in trying to meet my needs with homosexual behaviour.

A lot of my recovery was about acknowledging the deep wounds, hurts and deprivations of my past, and seeking God's help to deal with them. To a very large degree, it was also a matter of growing up emotionally and psychologically.

After I came back to God, I stopped drinking, using drugs and engaging in promiscuous sex. Looking back now, I realise I used these things, unknowingly, to keep pain submerged. While it was submerged, I didn't have to feel it, face it, or deal with it. Stopping these things enabled the pain to surface, and it also enabled me to feel it and deal with it appropriately, instead of keeping it anaesthetised and repressed. Some of these feelings were intense, and sometimes the intensity was very frightening.

Gradually, and over time, I became aware that God wanted to touch and heal certain things. Some of these things were the result of my sinful choices, and I had to take responsibility for these. They needed to be confessed to God as sin because I needed and wanted his forgiveness. For example, I was not responsible for the abuse I experienced growing up, but I *was* responsible for my *reactions* to what happened.

I also became more aware of the physical and emotional deprivation I had experienced in my relationship with my father. As I observed some of the healthy relationships between men and their children in my church, I sometimes wondered what would have happened if my father had shown me that sort of love and affection – would I have gone looking for it in a gay bar? Of course, I saw the other side as well, in that many of the men didn't relate to their children at all. They were so busy 'doing the Lord's work' that they didn't have time for their family.

The name-calling, or external labelling, I received when I was growing up also had to be dealt with. Many times I was called 'poofter', 'pansy', 'queer', and so on, and I felt pain as well as a lot of anger about this. Sometimes this anger was so intense it frightened me. I remember being amazed at how something which happened so long ago still had power to hurt and cause such strong feelings in the present. In actual fact, I was feeling the pain that I had repressed for many years. At the time, I didn't realise that feeling this pain and being able to acknowledge it was a valuable part of the healing process. I just felt as though the wounds were still raw after all those years. I needed to move on and extend forgiveness to the people who were responsible for the labelling

I had received. This took time, but one by one they were forgiven, and I released them to God.

I also had a great deal of growing up to do. Some of my responses to people and to being hurt were childish, and over the years I have faced the fact that sometimes I behaved very immaturely. For example, my desire for instant gratification – wanting what I wanted, when I wanted it – was not an attribute of maturity. Self-pity has also been something that comes very easily to me at times.

God has helped me deal with many of these stunted character traits. In my own journey, and over years of ministering to people who struggle with unwanted same-sex attraction, I have come to realise that there are many who are emotionally and relationally immature. I believe that 'growing up' – or maturing emotionally and relationally – is a significant part of the healing process.

As I moved further along in my journey, my relationships with other Christian men grew in importance and value. Apart from friendship, some of these men provided me with the good role models I needed, which my father hadn't provided. These friendships were firmly based on mutuality. None of the men I was close to treated me as their 'project'. I would have found this extremely offensive, and no relationship would have been possible if they had attempted to make me a 'good deed'. I wanted friendship and respect as a person; I did not want to be patronised and paraded as a 'good work'.

Over the years, I believe God revealed to me what needed to be dealt with, and as he did, I tried my best to deal with it. This included forgiving when and where necessary, professional counselling at various times, and specific prayer. Much later, when Christian books became available on the subject of homosexuality, I read as much as I could about it. As I gained understanding and insight, I was able to apply whatever things were appropriate for me.

Much of my walk away from homosexuality has been simply living the Christian life. By that I mean reading the Bible, praying, resisting temptation, belonging to a church, meeting with other Christians –

just living the Christian life. There have been times when nothing very spectacular has been happening at all. I believe that to continually expect God to serve up miracles to us is a futile expectation. Some growth is just a slow and steady plod. I have been content to leave my process, as well as its timing, to God. There has also been an ongoing choice to be made: Will I stay with God and do it his way, or will I go back to what I was and try to do it my way?

Coming out of active homosexuality and growing beyond it has been a long and at times, a painful journey. But I now know and love God more because he has guided and walked through that change and growth process with me. I know just how kind, compassionate, gentle and caring he has been and continues to be with me.

Early on in my walk with God, I decided to be completely honest with him. I tried hard to avoid being false and sanctimonious. I also tried to avoid thinking in religious clichés. Nor was I interested in just 'polishing' my theology or holding God at arm's length. I wanted a *real* relationship with him. I needed to connect with him on an emotional level as well as an intellectual level. I have also always tried to keep in my mind that God is on *my* side. He is *for* me, *not* against me. All this has helped me to be able to express my feelings, hurts, questions, and much else to God in a straightforward way, without fear.

My recovery came through my relationship with God. Everything else was secondary to that. Reading, counselling, and support groups were at times very helpful and important, but not as important as spending time with God. It is an *absolutely* sure and certain way to grow.

My process of healing was complicated and delayed by marrying both too soon and for the wrong reasons. But even this was used by God in my process of growth, in that it forced me to work on things that needed to be faced and dealt with.

Have I been completely 'healed'? No, there are still areas in which I struggle. One of the main ones is the 'father deficit' I still feel at times. I recall a visit, made with my wife and another friend, to an older man, who was intelligent, well-spoken and very interesting to listen to. As well as being pleasant to be with, there was a gentleness about him which was lovely. As we sat and talked with him, I began to feel sad. I realised later that I was sad because he was just the sort of man I would have liked to have had as a father. The feelings stayed with me for days after the visit. God has done a lot of healing in this area, but obviously the healing has not been completed yet. Every now and then it still catches me unawares.

In more recent times I have become aware of another area of my life I missed out on completely. In a conversation with friends one night, the discussion turned to things people do that involve, to my way of thinking, a high degree of risk. We talked about people who climb the arch of the Sydney Harbour Bridge, sail alone around the world and take part in various other 'risky' adventures. I expressed the view that I just couldn't understand why people would take the risks involved in participating in such activities. I don't think anyone present understood what I was saying. I wasn't being critical; it just didn't compute in my head why people would choose to do those things. One of the men present became quite frustrated and angry as he tried to tell me that these things were 'normal'. 'Well, they aren't normal to me,' I replied.

The next day, as I thought about the conversation, I wondered why I felt so unable to understand the people who took risks like the ones we had spoken about. I began to realise that this side of me – the more masculine, risk-taking side – was never encouraged or modelled and has therefore never developed. Growing up surrounded by women, I developed the more 'feminine' side of my nature. The more masculine side had been completely neglected. It was a breakthrough in my thinking to understand the 'why' of it. It doesn't make me want to change my interests or my personality, but it's good to have the understanding.

Speaking of recovery for the person who struggles with unwanted same-sex attraction, Alan Medinger comments:

> We no longer define ourselves by the narrow and constraining label of 'gay'. We become totally comfortable with our manhood or womanhood. Our identity as persons is no longer at war with the

> bodies that God has given us. We experience healing from many of the things in our past that set us up for homosexuality. Low self-esteem, sexual abuse, and past rejection by a parent or peers no longer have so much power over us ... With our eyes no longer so focussed on our own gender, we start to appreciate the opposite sex in new and exciting ways ... The change in our sexual and non-sexual attractions has become sufficient to make possible our entering into a marriage that is full and complete in every way, including sexually.[15]

My healing was much more than just changing my lifestyle and stopping homosexual behaviour. That would be *abstinence*, not *healing*.

Let's have a look at the word healing. I know in some Christian circles the very word 'healing' is like waving a red rag at a bull. Once, whilst speaking about homosexuality at a meeting for clergy, I was asked to define the word 'healing'. I suspect the person who asked the question was irritated that I was using the word at all. I also had a hunch that he would have liked to have had a theological debate about the merits of healing, but I wasn't going to oblige him by going there. My answer to him was, 'Yes, I can give you a personal definition of healing. Once I was a promiscuous homosexual, who struggled with depression, drank excessively, used drugs frequently and felt miserable about the life I was leading. Now I am a happily married Christian man who is emotionally, spiritually and sexually fulfilled. I neither abuse drugs nor drink excessively and I have a life which is contented, fulfilled and very happy. I call that healing, don't you?' He said, 'Yes', and we moved on.

Some Christians don't believe God heals today, even though there is no evidence to support this point of view in the Bible. Another extreme I have heard some ministers teach, is that everything is healed when we are converted. Of course, this is nonsense. If it *were* true, there wouldn't be any new Christians wearing glasses.

I am aware many people would be outraged to hear that a homosexual would have a need for healing. 'We were born this way, who are you to suggest we would want to be any other way?'

My own view of healing is that God is the God of all flesh, and if he chooses to heal, he chooses to heal. I have experienced enough healing in my own life not to doubt the veracity of this. I have prayed for healing for others and have seen God heal in some, but not all, instances. Why some were healed and some were not is something I do not understand, but it would not stop me praying for healing for someone who asked me to.

One experience of healing I remember was a time when Truda's mother was suffering from a ganglion on her wrist which was causing her difficulties. Her doctor told her that she needed an operation, and I can remember thinking that it would be a miracle if she came through the anaesthetic.

After Truda's Dad and she divorced, she had started attending a church; however, after she told them she was a divorced person she was told she wasn't welcome there. After this experience, understandably, her attitude to the church wasn't a favourable one. I took a risk though, and said to her that I believed God could heal people and that I had experienced some healing in my own life. Would she be willing to let us pray for her? She agreed. We then prayed, and she was healed. Over the next couple of days the ganglion just disappeared.

Another time, Truda's mother was in a great deal of pain with shingles. Her doctor warned her that she would be in pain for a long time. She could only take a mild pain killer, and she told us in despair that she just didn't think she could cope with the pain she was in.

Again we asked if she would let us pray with her, and again she agreed. We simply asked God to come to her by the power of his Holy Spirit and to heal her. We waited, and after a while she told us that the pain had ceased in a portion of her body. She still felt it in other parts of her body, but a section of her was now pain-free. We prayed again, and she said that another section was pain-free. We prayed a third time, and this time she said all the pain had gone.

After we thanked God for what he had done, I said to her that she must realise now that Jesus really cared about her in a personal way. She agreed. I then asked her if she would like to ask him for forgiveness of her sins and to come into her life to be her Saviour. She said yes. We prayed, and she experienced the biggest healing of her life – the healing of her soul. She went on with God until her death a few years later.

I could never say that God doesn't heal today, as I have experienced it in my own life and seen it in the lives of others.

From my perspective, I find it very sad that the option of change, recovery or healing for the homosexual person who wants it, is not presented more clearly by the church. These days, there is a wealth of excellent material available for Christians who wish to deal with their unwanted same-sex attraction. There are now also many 'ex-gay' ministries worldwide who are working with Christians who want change and healing. I thank God that people who desire to change are not in the same situation that I was in all those years ago with so few, or no resources.

Over many years I have come to realise just how many Christians are struggling with unwanted homosexual feelings. I am also aware of how many conflicting attitudes there are about it within the church. Sadly, I have also realised just how ill-equipped, and sometimes unwilling, the church is to deal with it. The ignorance about the subject is frightening. Take, for example, the man who was told if he married, his homosexuality would disappear. It didn't. Or the person who was told what was really needed was deliverance from the demon of homosexuality. Women have been told if they looked more feminine, wore lipstick and dresses, and found themselves 'a real man' they would not have a sexuality problem. But perhaps the award for absurdity should go to the person who said that homosexuality was caused by people eating take-away chicken. This person believed that homosexuality was caused by female hormones fed to chickens.

Ignorance abounds about homosexuality, particularly regarding its causes and the fact that people *can* change if that is their choice.

CHAPTER 7

The Years Restored

'His thoughts said, But the lost years, what of them?
His Father said, I will restore to thee the years that the locust hath eaten, the cankerworm and the caterpillar and the palmer worm. I know the names of all the insects and worms which have devoured thy beauty and thy power. I will deal with them all, and cause thee to help others in danger of like injury, so shall thy years be restored.'

Amy Carmichael, *His Thought Said ... His Father Said ...*[16]

It was Saturday June 15, 1985. I slept very little the night before because of a really atrocious cold. I dosed myself with so many ephedrine tablets that I had been awake for most of the night. Two friends would be arriving in a few hours and then we would all take the short drive to the church where I would be married for the second time. It was certainly a challenge trying to make myself appear reasonable when I felt and looked like death warmed up.

It was just a little under nine years since I left homosexuality. A lot of water had passed under the bridge since then, and now here I was about to begin another part of my life. I was going to marry one of the most beautiful, if not *the* most beautiful, woman I had ever met and I was as sick as a dog!

I met Truda seven months before in church. I thought she was lovely the first time I saw her, and I wanted to get to know her. Our friendship developed very quickly. We had lots in common and spent hours talking together. I'm not sure what her friends thought of all this. Here was this ex-missionary and an ex-gay, and it was starting to look serious.

It didn't take me long to realise that I was very, very keen on her. I didn't know what would happen, as I was frightened of the risks involved in another relationship. After all, my history in the area of relationships wasn't exactly wonderful, or at least that's the way I saw it. I was also fearful for her. What if this relationship turned out to be a disaster as the former ones had? How would that affect her? I thought much too much of her to want her to be hurt in any way. However, the more I grew to know and to love Truda, and the more I prayed about it, the less the risks seemed to be. In fact, I had reached the point where my life would be very empty indeed without her.

I had never been able to look at just any woman and lust after her. I just didn't seem to function like that. I read later that this is really quite normal for men who have come out of homosexuality. I quote Alan Medinger:

> One of the great distresses that the Christian overcomer feels has to do with his lack of sexual attraction to women. He wants this to change, and before he has thought about it much, his assumption may be that being sexually attracted to women is really the beginning and the end of what ex-gay ministry is all about. In fact, the majority of Christian men who come to Regeneration[17] do seem to want to exchange their homosexual lust for heterosexual lust. They know that most men struggle with heterosexual lust, and they want to be like most men. It sounds perfectly logical until we realize that God is not in the business of giving out lust. He is not interested in our exchanging one form of sin for another. So what does happen? What can the man who is growing into manhood reasonably expect to experience?
>
> Most men overcoming homosexuality find that a strong sexual attraction to women does not arise until that one special person comes into his life, and then the sexual attraction flows naturally out of loving her. It might go something like this. You know a woman and like her, and you are healed enough so that you can truly appreciate those womanly things that make her different. You start to get to know her better, and the desire to be with her increases and increases, finally blossoming into romantic love. As this happens you want to be close to her, to hold her, and finally you want to be totally one with her - in mind, spirit, and body. Your desire for union with her has flowed naturally and beautifully out of loving her.[18]

This was the way it was for me then, and it still is.

From the start, Truda and I were both completely open with each other about our lives and the things we had faced and dealt with. I wanted this relationship to work, and for that to happen it had to be built on trust. Honesty and openness about my past was fundamental to that trust.

Truda wasn't at all fazed by my history. It was obvious to both of us that after a lot of very solid work in the nine years since I left homosexuality, same-sex attraction was no longer something I struggled with. The many years of freedom from homosexual attraction, as well as the freedom from involvement in emotionally dependent relationships with other men, were proof of this for me.

Truda and I became Christians at about the same time, but unlike me, she had stayed with God since her conversion. Where I left him for fifteen years, she was faithful in her commitment and walk with him.

She trained as a nurse, and after giving herself time to gain experience as well as some extra qualifications, she went to East Africa as a medical missionary. She served there for seven years in a mission hospital in Mvumi, Tanzania. These were exciting and fulfilling years for her. As well as working as a midwife and delivering many babies, both African and missionary, she was also involved in training nurses. She set up a new maternity section at the hospital, including a premature baby nursery. Truda also spent a number of months as assistant matron and acting matron during the tense time when Tanzania and Uganda were at war. One of her worst experiences was dealing with a major cholera outbreak at that time. One of the 'highs' of her time in Africa was completing a Bible school course on cassette with a group of Christian nurses. What very different paths we had taken.

Truda's parents separated and divorced when she was in her twenties, and since then she had had little contact with her father. In 1979 she decided to return to Australia to try to get to know him better and improve her relationship with him.

She had had her own struggles to deal with and grow through. Here is part of her journey in her own words.

'My story is not one of struggling with same-sex attraction. However,

having worked with a number of women dealing with these issues, I have come to realise that there are many similarities between their relationship with their fathers and my relationship with mine.

Early memories of Dad are of a gentle, always polite, emotionally distant man. He was a good provider and tried his best to care for Mum and me, his only child. However, I remember very little apart from a goodnight kiss, in the way of physical affection or contact. The only other significant male in those childhood years was a beloved Grandpa who died when I was nine. Both men were gentle, practical, but passive men who were dominated by my mother and my grandmother.

During my teenage years Mum and Dad were separated off and on, and I was at a boarding school for girls. My mother started to run Dad down as well as all men in general. She was very bitter as the marriage disintegrated and ended in divorce. After my conversion to Christ at sixteen, I remember being convicted of my fear and hatred of my Dad and of all men. I realised I needed to repent of this, and I asked God for a love for my mostly absent father, and rejected my mother's attitudes.

At boarding school, mostly before all this acrimonious and bitter stuff, I had a friendship with a boy from my brother school. We attended the same dance classes, and managed to sneakily partner each other even though we were supposed to change partners constantly. Apart from this there were no other relationships with the opposite sex. I felt very insecure in my femininity. I was scared of relating to guys and felt totally inadequate and very timid around them.

I saw Dad very infrequently as a teenager, and then not at all for seven years up to 1971, the year before I entered missionary training college. My relationship with God held me through very difficult times with my mother, who was not only bitter, but also very opposed to my Christian faith and missionary calling.

My sense of inferiority, unworthiness, and insecurity continued through to my mid-thirties, when I returned from the mission field.

Having told a little about my relationship with my Dad, I would like to relate briefly some of the ways in which God has changed me and repaired the damage.

I had counselling regarding my family mess after my return from Tanzania. I worked with a particularly gifted male counsellor who affirmed me as a woman and with whom I was able to build trust – the first male I had ever trusted, I think. I felt as if I was going through puberty in my thirties. God dealt with all sorts of emotional and affirmation gaps, and I grew much closer in my relationship with him.

At the same time I was involved with a Christian dance/drama group. One of the unexpected spin offs of this was that through the many movement and drama workshops I attended I was able to get in touch with the deep painful stuff I needed to deal with. I grieved the deep losses from inadequate parenting before God and received much comfort and resolution. Many times the scriptures brought truth and comfort to me in those tough and painful times.

As well, all through the years a very special Christian couple, Ken and Gloria Short, loved me and accepted me into their family and thus showed me what a normal Christian family life was like. Although they were too young to be my parents, their love, acceptance and warmth brought me what I had never known in my own family.

My relationship with God, while a constant and daily one since teenage years, was deeply affected by the charismatic renewal we experienced in Tanzania. I became much more free and emotionally engaged with my God. I knew my need for emotional healing was enormous, and I knew he was the only one who could do it. I earnestly sought his healing. I realised at some point that I saw God through the filter of my own father – emotionally distant, passive, and as I perceived it, not really interested in me. My sense of unworthiness pervaded my relationship with him. However, God showed me that he is my Father God and Dad was a broken human being with his own deficits. They are completely different. I remember being totally overwhelmed as I let the truth of God's father love wash over me. I have learnt much about his character as I have read the scriptures and looked at Jesus' character and qualities. I have found proof of God's constant and perfect love over many years.

As healing occurred, I pursued a relationship with Dad. A deeper understanding and reconciliation happened between us. We talked of *many things, and I grew to respect and love him more deeply, while recognising many of the past deficits could never be made up between us. We could work with what we had in the present. I did in fact have 22 years at the end of his long life in a much better relationship with him. He acknowledged more than once how much he regretted leaving me to my mother during my teenage years, but did so because he thought it was the best thing. Little did he realise the enormous damage this caused. Many times, as I have understood new painful things about our relationship, I have forgiven him and released him to God.*

The most wonderful outcome of this healing journey has been coming into a deep security and delight in my femininity and a confidence in relating to men. The constant feelings of unworthiness and inferiority have gone. I came to strongly desire a relationship with a man and also felt attraction to men. God is pretty marvellous in the way he does things, as he has given me Chris, who is the most affirming and affectionate and adoring husband imaginable. The constancy and joy in that relationship has been a further step in my healing process, which still goes on to this day. I hope I will always be in a process of change and growth with my Father God.'

Truda's mother once told me a lovely story about something Truda did when she was about three years old. Truda is a redhead, with the typical fair skin of a redhead. From an early age her mother constantly emphasised to her the importance of wearing a hat and keeping out of the sun because she was so fair. One day her mother came out into the garden to find that Truda had picked all the heads off the flowers in a bed of marigolds. When she asked her why she had done this, Truda took her over to a large tree that was growing in the garden and showed her where she had carefully laid out the flowers in very neat rows under the tree. She had done this, she explained, because she didn't want the flowers to get sunburnt.

During our first year of married life, we took an extended holiday in Europe and enjoyed exploring it together. It was my first time in Europe, although Truda had been before. We had a wonderful time exploring places like Lucerne, Rome, Florence, Venice, Paris and London together. We caught up with a few of Truda's friends who also served in Tanzania. We saw a great deal of England and loved every minute of it.

We came home and settled down into the routine of work and church. As we became more involved in our local church and got to know people better, we found that some of these people were confiding in us as well as asking us to pray with them. As we both enjoyed people, listening and praying with them seemed a very natural thing to do. The minister in our church must have recognised some sort of ability in us, because he asked us to train others to pray for people in the same way. In time we had a team of people who were able to pray for others after the service on a Sunday night. Many people wanted to be able to apply the teaching they had heard in the service, so they came forward for prayer. There were others who wanted prayer for various things that were happening in their lives, so they came for prayer as well. We saw some great things happen as a result of those times of ministry.

Martin Luther has been quoted as saying that 'Marriage is God's best way of explaining himself'. I understand what he meant. In my own marriage I have learned so much about love, acceptance, loyalty and faithfulness. It is through the love of my wife that I have come to know *God's* love for me in an even deeper and more complete way. Without her love, encouragement and support, I wouldn't have grown as much as a person, nor would I have experienced as much healing as I have. Truda has been a wonderful friend, lover and companion, and without her my journey would have been a very much poorer one than the one I have experienced.

CHAPTER 8

Speaking Out

'I have told all your people about your justice.
I have not been afraid to speak out, as you, O Lord, well know.
I have not kept the good news of your justice hidden in my heart;
I have talked about your faithfulness and saving power.
I have told everyone in the great assembly of your unfailing love and faithfulness.'

Psalm 40:9–10

One morning I was praying and asking God what it was he specifically wanted me to do. I suppose I had heard God 'speak' to me a few times in my life. An example was the time, mentioned earlier, when I was prompted to visit Mrs Gray, the old lady who had lived in the apartment below mine. On that occasion I was obedient to what I thought God was saying, and it may have resulted in her coming to him before she died. Even so, I am not the type of person who runs around saying 'God told me this' or 'God told me that'. I didn't trust that sort of thing, and I had many reservations about it. Nevertheless, this morning, as I waited on God, I felt him say quite distinctly, 'I want you to preach the gospel to gays.' I did not hear an audible voice. It was an impression of those words, but a very strong impression.

This wasn't something I was expecting, and it certainly wasn't something I wanted, so I knew I hadn't made it up. Homosexuality! I had had enough of that to last me a lifetime. And what exactly did 'preach the gospel to gays' mean? Was I expected to go up to the gay area of Sydney with a Bible under my arm and evangelise gays on the streets? If that was what God meant, I didn't know how I was going to obey. It was something I felt I could not possibly do.

'This is not real,' I told myself. But even as I said the words, I knew in my heart it was from God.

I told Truda, and she didn't seem to be shocked by the idea at all. To test this 'call' out, I then told a mutual friend. Her reply was, 'Oh yes Chris, I can see that so clearly. Of course God would want that. And who would be as well qualified as you to do something like that?' She spoke as if it was the most obvious and natural thing in the world. She was someone whom I respected and trusted, and although I had mixed feelings about her response I certainly took it seriously.

In time, it seemed to be a more reasonable idea than I had first thought, and I began making enquiries. However, I was not surprised to find out that there were no ministries to homosexuals in Sydney.

As I got more used to the idea, I remembered that many years before I had once prayed to God and asked him to use me to help people who struggled in the same way I did. The prayer was sincere, but over time, and with so much happening in my life, I had forgotten all about it. God obviously hadn't.

Truda finally tracked down an Australian pastor who had trained with a US-based ministry that helped Christians who were dealing with unwanted same-sex attraction. This was a breakthrough, as it was the first ministry we had heard about which was offering something. It sounded like it was just the sort of thing we were looking for. After we had met and talked, he invited us to be a part of the first run-through of the program, but it was conditional on us agreeing to lead a small group for him the next time he ran it. This was the beginning of our experience with a program called 'Living Waters'.

Andy Comisky is an ex-homosexual who designed and wrote the course, which he describes as an 'in-depth counselling, teaching and discipleship series'. At the time we used it, the program ran for twenty weeks and was a good resource. The teaching was on tape, and as well as listening to the tapes, there were several books which were required reading for the participants.

Participants in the course were divided into small groups of about six men per group. The group I was in, which met once a week, was made up of Christians from very different backgrounds, all of whom were there because they wanted to deal with their unwanted same-sex attraction.

As the other men in my group shared their stories, I quickly recognised many of the same things I had dealt with myself.

The meeting began with a time of worship, moved on to a time of teaching, and then ended in small groups, where we shared and were prayed for. About half way through the course, the leader of one of the groups left. There was a reshuffle, which left me leading my group. Of course, this cut short my process as a participant. It was also far too early for me to be in a leadership position, as I was not fully familiar with the material.

The time passed very quickly, and before I knew it the next course was ready to begin. This time I had a co-leader, which felt more comfortable. However, as was the case for the first course, I had no choice about who was allocated to my group. This was a problem for me, because the men in the group I had been allocated to lead were at very different stages in their Christian faith as well as in their process of dealing with their unwanted same sex attraction. Some were very new Christians and therefore much of the group time was spent in explaining basic Christian doctrine and beliefs. There were also differences in our beliefs. For example, some of the men believed that homosexual feelings were demonic and needed to be 'cast out', whereas I had a different view. Many of the men were in various stages of grief about their lives and my way was to listen, acknowledge the feelings and encourage them to deal with their feelings in a healthy psychological way – not cast the feeling out as a demon. Naming emotions as demons stopped the men from taking responsibility for their own feelings and dealing with them in a mature and adult way. I am not asserting that the realm of the demonic does not exist – in my view the Bible shows that it does quite clearly. However, it is my opinion in this situation that the feelings these men were experiencing were just that – feelings, not demons.

Not long after the second course finished, Truda and I decided to go to the US and do the training with Andy Comisky, to better enable us to lead the program. This involved doing the full course at an accelerated rate, and making sure we dealt with our own issues before we were put into leadership positions.

It was interesting and challenging; we were a part of a group of people who had mostly left a life of homosexuality and now wanted to reach out to others in the same situation.

We ran this program in our home for about eight years. What a history that sentence holds!

During this time, we saw a number of people successfully deal with issues relating to their unwanted same-sex attraction. We also saw people grow in their understanding and love of God. At the end of each course, we would ask people what had been the most valuable aspect for them. Most said it was the love and acceptance they felt, as well as being part of a group of people where they were able to share openly about the deep hurts in their lives. Many times we were told that their shame, as well as the isolation they had known, had lifted for them. We are still in touch with some of these people today. I have often wished there had been something similar to this course available when I came out of homosexuality. It would have been such a valuable help and would have reduced my isolation greatly.

Running such groups can be exciting and rewarding. It is also demanding and tiring work, especially when one has a full-time day job. After eight years, and feeling quite exhausted, I started to pray that if God wanted me to work in this ministry long-term, he would provide the finances for me to do it without having to work during the day as well.

No church was interested in what we were doing, even though there were many Christian friends who were individually supportive of us. We didn't know if it was too hot an issue for the church, or if they just did not care sufficiently about this people group to fund a ministry of this type.

One day I received a telephone call from Dr David Peterson, who was at that time a lecturer at Moore Theological College in Sydney. He invited us to come and meet with a group of people who were interested in setting up some sort of ministry to Christians in Sydney who were struggling with unwanted same-sex attraction.

Finally, someone in the church was interested. We had been struggling with the lack of interest from the leadership of our own church and with the isolation of the work. We were also both working full-time in other jobs, in addition to the work with our small groups. Furthermore, we were struggling with 'compassion fatigue' from being constantly surrounded by people in pain.

This was the state of mind we were in when we went to the meeting. Thankfully, this was a group of people who saw the need. They realised that something needed to be done for the many Christians who were struggling – people who did not want to embrace a gay identity, but were having difficulties with their sexuality and wanted help. Even though we had looked for this sort of interest from the church for many years, now it was finally here we were both too tired to be excited by it. David's group had heard about what we were doing and wanted to know if we could help them to set up something similar.

We met with them regularly for several months, and over that time I shared about my experience in coming out of homosexuality as well as our experiences with group work. These people recognised how tired we were and put no pressure or demands on us; it was refreshing to be with people who respected the work we had been doing. In fact, the gentle acceptance and encouragement we were shown was a restoring experience for us both.

David was very keen to have some sort of public meeting. He felt that this was necessary, in order to generate interest and support for this type of ministry. I was asked if I would be willing to tell my story publicly.

It is one thing to share in a small group where it is safe, but it's quite another to share in a public meeting where anyone can come and hear. Was I ready? Who would now know about my former life as a practising homosexual? If people knew, was it really an issue? Also, there were two people involved in this decision, Truda and myself, and we both needed to ask ourselves some serious questions. How would sharing publicly affect our families and our lives? Were we willing to sacrifice our privacy? So many questions to think through, and we were the only ones who could make the final decision, as it was *our* lives that would be affected, not anyone else's. After talking it through, we finally came to the conclusion that if only one person was helped, it had to be worth the cost of speaking publicly. And anyway, how could I face God at some stage in the future, knowing that I had chosen not to speak when I could?

After one very small meeting at Moore Theological College, where I was interviewed about homosexuality, David arranged a public meeting at a church in Oxford Street, Sydney.

St Matthias is a well-known evangelical church with a large congregation and a very successful ministry to many in this city. It is also geographically on the edge of the gay area in Sydney. Although I had taught and led small groups, I had not done any public speaking on this scale before. Would people actually be interested in what I had to say? Would anyone bother to come? What if I had a heart attack when I got up to speak? Worse still, what if I made a total mess of it? The thought of making a mess of it was far worse than the thought of having a heart attack!

As I sat down to write the talk, I found the words came very quickly. In fact, it flowed. I knew exactly what I wanted to say, and I also knew how I wanted to say it. I felt nervous, but also very excited.

Finally, the night arrived. The church was crowded. Many of our friends came, as well as some of the people from our previous groups and others we had contact with. There were also many people there whom we had never seen before. Just as I was about to start, I noticed a large group of gay men come in and sit at the back of the church. This was it; I was probably going to be, at the very least, verbally abused by these guys.

I was surprised to find that as I stood in front of the microphone, I felt strangely calm. I told my story: how I had become a Christian; how I went into homosexuality; how, in time, I became disillusioned; how I had left it; and since then, the journey of change and healing God had taken me on. The stillness of the audience was unnerving. What were these people thinking?

When I finished, there was a burst of applause I will never forget. I went cold all over, and then as the applause continued, I knew that it was accompanied by a great deal of love and acceptance. I also realised that what I had said had obviously struck a chord with these people.

Within a week, David Peterson rang to ask me if I would come and work for their ministry.

Over the next week or so, as I thought about that night, I slowly came to the realisation that if the gospel was the good news about Jesus Christ, as well as forgiveness, freedom and healing from sin, then I had preached the gospel to those people that night.

Truda and I went on to work with Liberty Christian Ministries – the name the ministry was given – as their pastoral workers for eight years. Sadly for us, David wasn't around for very long, as he went to head up a theological college in England.

During our eight years, I spoke publicly about homosexuality at countless churches and lectured at several theological colleges, including speaking annually at Moore Theological College in Sydney.

One of the more unusual places I spoke at was Long Bay Correctional Complex. Some of the men in my church were involved in a prison ministry, and they suggested I speak there. My initial reaction was to say 'no', but after thinking about it, I accepted the invitation.

The prison is a grim stone building which was opened on the eve of World War 1. The meeting was only for men – female inmates were moved to Mulawa Correctional Centre in 1969. I was nervous, as I hadn't a clue as to what type of reception I was going to get. However, things went well; the prisoners listened attentively and asked many questions after I had finished speaking.

Whilst working with Liberty, I also edited a book of stories about people who struggled with homosexuality. In addition, I led many support groups for both men and women who were seeking help with their unwanted same-sex attraction, as well as support groups for people who were affected by the homosexuality of a loved one.

CHAPTER 9

Understanding Homosexuality

'One of the best things the church can do – across the board – is to begin to understand the causes of homosexuality. It produces compassion and identification rather than aversion and rejection in conservatives, and – if liberals can bring themselves to do it – can help them see that the desire to help homosexuals change does not necessarily have its origins in rejection and lack of love. It does not mean conservatives have to agree with or accept homosexuality as a lifestyle.'

Briar Whitehead, *Craving for Love*[19]

We are now living in an age where many people believe there is nothing wrong with homosexuality. It is commonplace to see homosexual characters portrayed in movies, plays and on television, and advertisers use homoerotic images to sell their products. It has been 'normalised' by the world, as well as some parts of the church, as just another option we have about our sexuality.

Anyone who is 'politically incorrect' by challenging or questioning homosexuality is labelled as 'homophobic'. A phobia could be defined as an exaggerated fear or dread which can control a person's mind. This is hardly the same as challenging or expressing a different point of view. Yet 'homophobic' is now used to describe the person who either has a negative response to homosexuality or who doesn't immediately and fully endorse the 'gay' agenda.[20]

Unfortunately, much of what we hear in the media and see in movies about homosexuality is misleading. One example is the selective use of statistics to support the assertion that an estimated 10% of the population is gay.[21]

Another example is the message that people are born homosexual and they can't change. Briar and Neil Whitehead have this to say in their book *My Genes Made Me Do It!*

Here is a very basic truth. There is nothing fixed or final about the

> homosexual orientation and its natural expression, homosexual behaviour. No one has to stay homosexual or lesbian, in orientation or behaviour, if he or she doesn't want to and informed support is available. No politician, church leader, church member, judge, counsellor, homosexual person, or friend or family of a homosexual person, needs to feel forced into a position on homosexuality based on the apparent immutability of the homosexual orientation. Homosexuality is not inborn, not genetically dictated, not immutable. Nor, for that matter, is heterosexuality or any other human behaviour. In fact, our genes do not make us do anything. Whether it's homosexuality, a foul temper, bedwetting, or addiction to chocolate, our genes have very little to do with it.[22]

Many in the gay community react with shock and disbelief to the suggestion that they have a choice about their sexuality. The idea that a choice exists is potentially a very threatening concept. Some have struggled for years before accepting the label of 'gay' in their lives, and there are many who cannot remember a time when they weren't attracted to a person of the same sex. This would lead them to the belief that they were born gay. Research has shown that the paths we take in life are laid down at a very early age, so it's therefore not surprising that the message from the gay community – that a person is 'born gay' – is accepted at face value. So, to be confronted with the claim that a homosexual can change is – in many cases – ridiculed and not believed.[23] Furthermore, some who have come out of the gay community have gone back into it, hence the term 'ex-ex-gay'. This contributes to the general attitude of disbelief within this group regarding the concept of change.

It follows that people have been convinced that anyone who has a sexual attraction to a person of the same sex should proclaim themselves as 'gay' and rapidly move on to fully embrace a 'gay' identity. As a consequence, many Christian men and women with same-sex attraction believe they are powerless to do anything about it.

However, the truth is there are many Christians who will *never* act upon their same-sex attraction. They have chosen to live their lives according to what God has said in his word. For some this has meant celibacy, whilst others have gone on to experience happy, contented and fulfilled marriages with a person of the opposite sex. I am one of those people. These choices are something the gay community is determined not to accept[24], yet this same community expects that people accept without question the choices and decisions *they* have made for their lives.

For sixteen years I worked with other Christians who chose not to embrace active homosexuality but, sadly, many of these people have chosen never to disclose their unwanted same-sex attraction or their journey of recovery. This is a tragedy because a great many people would certainly benefit from their honesty, openness and a clear testimony of the truth of their journey.

Martin Hallett is an ex-homosexual who for many years has worked in a ministry in Britain called True Freedom Trust. He has had years of experience supporting Christians who are struggling with unwanted same-sex attraction and says:

> There are probably nearly as many Christians with homosexual feelings who do not believe that homosexual sex is right for Christians as there are those who are advocating its acceptance. Apart from one or two people like myself, the majority of these 'celibate homosexuals' (for want of a better phrase) are silent. They fear rejection from their (mainly evangelical) friends, but they also feel very uncomfortable with liberal views and believe that 'gay Christians' will not understand or accept them either ... The majority have been Christians for a long time, and some are church leaders. They are men, women, married, single, old, and young. If only their voice was heard, if only they could be encouraged to speak out, I believe that the church situation, its witness, and ministry, would be vastly different. Perhaps there would even be less of a risk of major splits and divisions in denominations debating the issues of homosexuality.[25]

Martin Hallett has chosen to be a voice encouraging truth and openness. One can only hope more people will be encouraged to follow his lead.

* * *

For the sake of a better understanding, let me begin by making a generalisation and describing homosexuality as three different groups of people.

In the first group we have the gay community, which includes those who have chosen active homosexuality as their lifestyle. Many have been hurt by the church and feel they have no place in the body of Christ. This belief would be enforced by the behaviour of some Christians, as well as what the media says about the church's attitudes to homosexuality. In the second group of people we have those who are proclaiming themselves as Christians, with a foot in both the 'gay' community as well as the church. In the third group we have the many Christians who are struggling with unwanted same-sex desires, in an environment – the church – that doesn't necessarily understand either the condition or the process involved for those who want change. These people – both male and female – have made a definite decision that they do not want to be practicing homosexuals. This was the group of people I worked with for sixteen years.

When discussing homosexuality with a gay friend or relative, I believe it is important to let them vent their frustrations or hurts concerning the church. A person needs to be able to express those hurts, be heard, and have the hurt acknowledged.

Where the church *has* been wrong in its attitudes to homosexuals – and it *has* in some parts – we Christians need to be able to admit this, repent, and if appropriate and given the opportunity, apologise. We also need to learn to listen to people without becoming defensive. Too often we are quick to speak and slow to listen, when the Bible tells us to practice the opposite. If people have been hurt by Christians, let's listen and acknowledge their hurt. When people have had the opportunity to ventilate their hurt, empty it out, and have it acknowledged in some way, they may then be in a better place to actually hear what we have to say.

If we are sharing about Christianity, I believe it's important to remember that we are trying to introduce people to the Lord Jesus Christ, not present them with a moral code. We need to remember that one doesn't have to clean up a person's sex life before they can be introduced to Jesus. If the person gives their life to Jesus, he will help them get their sexuality on track if needed. And we can be confident that he will do that with a great deal more skill and sensitivity than we can.

Many Christians think that they need to talk people out of homosexuality. I don't believe that is our role. We are told to witness about Jesus, and that is what we should be doing. Share what the Lord has done in our *own* lives. Share how he died so they can know God as Father. Tell them their sins can be forgiven. Tell them they can have eternal life. Share the *important* things with them.

When the subject of what the Bible says about homosexuality inevitably comes up, share with them that as a Christian, we have chosen to be obedient to what God has said in his word about sex. God doesn't hate homosexuals, and it is important that the person we are sharing with understands this. Let us discuss sexuality and what the Bible says about it in the light of *all* sexual behaviour, not just the bits about homosexuality.

Sex is a gift from God, and the Bible provides guidelines about sex. This is not because God wants to deprive us of pleasure; rather, he knows how his gift works best and how it can bring us true happiness and fulfilment.

If a person chooses to live their life by what the Bible teaches, then that means sex is to be within a marriage between a man and a woman. The Bible forbids adultery and fornication, and that means immorality – either heterosexual or homosexual – is not what God intended or condones. Christians who are single practice chastity out of their love for God and because they want to be obedient to what the Bible teaches.

One important point, sometimes forgotten, is that God doesn't expect us to live our Christian lives in our own strength. He has given us his Holy Spirit to empower, transform, and strengthen us to live in obedience. People need to hear that they are not alone: they have the Holy Spirit as a constant companion to help them on their journey.

Not everyone, either heterosexual or ex-homosexual, will end up married. For the Christian who wants to live according to what the Bible teaches, that means singleness. Marriage is no more exalted a state than singleness. Either state will need the Holy Spirit to help us with lots of wisdom, love, self-discipline and whatever else is needed to be a mature and loving Christian.

Bishop Glenn Davies sums up succinctly what the Bible teaches in this way:

> The evidence of the New Testament affirms the creation intentions for humanity as set forth in the Old Testament. Man and woman, as image bearers of God are created for sexual union in the context of marriage, which is the lifelong, exclusive union between a male and a female. While marriage is the norm, not everyone will enjoy the benefit of being married. Some will remain single, either by choice or circumstances. Moreover, the New Testament countenances no provision for any sexual activity outside of marriage, whether that activity be heterosexual or homosexual in nature. The prohibitions on homosexuality are not limited merely to cultic homosexuality or promiscuous homosexuality. Rather, Paul's condemnation of homosexual practice appears absolute. It is against nature for two women to be involved in sexual intercourse, as it is for two men. In fact, Paul declares that such behaviour excludes one from an inheritance in the kingdom of God. However, this is not to suggest that homosexual behaviour is somehow more heinous than other sins. For all unrepented sin excludes one from God's kingdom. In this regard, homosexual activity is just one of a number of sins which are inconsistent and incompatible with the Christian life. The New Testament, accordingly, does not countenance the persecution of homosexuals that arises from a homophobia which does not recognise the validity and integrity of homosexuals as men and women made in the image of God.
>
> However, it is not impossible, according to the apostle Paul, for homosexuals to change their behaviour. The homosexual, by God's grace, can be set free from their sin and sanctified in the name of the Lord Jesus and in the power of the Holy Spirit. There is hope for

> those who want to live God's way. Fidelity to the teaching of the New Testament will always extend hope and mercy to all those who love God and seek to keep his commandments.[26]

If homosexuality is something we have had little to do with, it can be difficult to know what to say and what to recommend to people who disclose their same-sex attraction and want to be helped.

I don't believe people can be talked out of homosexuality; the motivation for change must come from within *them*. Some may have read a book or article that has given them hope for change. Some people may be ambivalent, or unsure if they really want help.

If ambivalence is present, a person *can* get to the place of making a committed decision with God to walk away from homosexuality. This can be done by an act of their will rather than by relying on their feelings.

There are roots and underlying causes of same-sex attraction. Many people have little understanding initially, but with reading and education, they begin to see that they have issues in common with other people experiencing same-sex attraction. There are many excellent books which deal with the causes and recovery from homosexuality, that are written from a Christian perspective (see the Resources section at the end of this book). I would strongly recommend reading some of these books to gain a deeper understanding of homosexuality.

It is very important for the person dealing with same-sex attraction to have friends who know and accept their struggle and pray for them. If we are one of these friends, it is important that the relationship is mutual. We need to be honest and self-revealing about ourselves. Most people do not want to be someone's 'good deed'.

Ideally, a support group will be a great place for growth. I believe the main components of a good support group are: Acceptance, Affirmation, and Accountability.

As readers will realise by now, people with same-sex attraction have issues, and very often, deep pain to deal with. This is much better dealt with in a professional counselling context.

The single most important thing for the person dealing with same-sex attraction is their relationship with Jesus Christ. Encouragement into a deep, intimate and honest relationship with God is a vital key to a person finding their true identity in Christ.

Praying with people is very important. Apart from the wonderful answers prayer brings, it helps to model the way in which we may speak to God honestly if they are not used to prayer.

Fellowship with others will break the isolation that is felt by many people, and it will help them to be integrated into the life of the church. The person may choose not to disclose their same-sex attraction in their church, and their decision – as well as their confidentiality – needs to be respected.

Finally, if we are helping or supporting someone struggling with unwanted same-sex attraction, it is good to remember that whilst the support we give may be of vital importance, the responsibility for the person's life and the choices they make remains with *them*, not *us*.

I recommend Exodus-affiliated ministries (see Resources section) for people who are looking for help in the area of homosexuality. Exodus will supply contact names of Christian ministries worldwide for people wishing to deal with unwanted same-sex attraction, as well as help for people who have been affected by the homosexuality of a loved one.

CHAPTER 10

The Pandemic of AIDS

'He jests at scars that never felt a wound.'
William Shakespeare, *Romeo and Juliet*

Truda and I were having dinner with some Christian friends. The conversation turned to homosexuality and in particular, HIV/AIDS. I was shocked when our hostess said, 'But don't you think they get exactly what they deserve?'

Over the next few weeks I kept coming back to her statement. I thought of the people I had known and in particular a friend of mine with whom I had been close.

Martin was about the same age as me and we were friends for many years. Our friendship was a close one although we were never involved sexually. We mixed with many of the same people and went to many of the same functions. I knew Martin's family just as he knew mine. We travelled overseas together and shared apartments on two separate occasions. When I decided to leave homosexuality I lost contact with many of the people I knew and Martin was one of these people.

One lunch time I met an acquaintance Martin and I both knew and in the course of our conversation I asked about some of those people, Martin being one of them. I was stunned when he told me that *all* of them were either HIV positive or had gone on to develop AIDS. I can remember walking back to work in absolute shock.

When I got back to the office I looked up Martin's sister's phone number and rang to see if and where I could make contact with him. She told me Martin was now living in another state but was coming to Sydney in the next few weeks. I gave her my telephone number and asked her to pass it on to her brother if she thought he would want to make contact again. I don't know if she gave him my message but I never heard from him.

I remember a support group Truda and I ran at one time. One of the men in the group told us he had lost over *thirty* friends who had died from AIDS. I don't know how one begins to cope with, or process, that sort of grief.

When I first heard about HIV/AIDS I had a blood test, which was negative. Even so, I have never lost sight of the fact that I have been extremely fortunate. I have not experienced personally either the disease or the grief and fear that would have enveloped the gay community with the onslaught of this devastating disease.

Naturally, I knew about HIV/AIDS from what I saw and heard in the media, and I also wondered from time to time who among my friends had become infected. However, because I moved on into a new life outside of the homosexual community, HIV/AIDS didn't have the immediate effect on me that it might have had, if I had stayed in that lifestyle.

This had now changed; the reality and ugliness of HIV/AIDS hit me in a new way when I was told of the eight people I knew personally who were affected. It was no longer something that was 'out there' – it was something that was happening to people I knew.

I thought again about our friend's comment – 'getting exactly what they deserved' – and felt sure there would be other Christians who would likewise see HIV/AIDS as God's judgment on practising homosexuals.[27] I also thought that if we all 'got exactly what we deserved', it would have been *us* on a cross instead of Jesus. That, to my mind, was the message of the gospel.

* * *

AIDS stands for Acquired Immune Deficiency Syndrome and HIV stands for the Human Immuno-deficiency Virus. The HIV virus can lie dormant in its human host for five to ten years or longer. When it does manifest itself, it attacks and damages the body's immune and nervous systems, making it defenceless against certain diseases.[28]

There are many theories about the origin of AIDS and HIV. Some believe it came from a promiscuous flight attendant, others believe it started with a suspect vaccination programme. There is even a conspiracy theory that the virus was man-made and deliberately designed and manufactured to kill large numbers of black and homosexual people. Although theories about the origins of HIV/AIDS still abound, it is now more commonly accepted that it developed as a spontaneous mutation of a virus which had long infected African monkeys.[29] The first recognised cases of AIDS occurred in the USA. A number of gay men in California and New York suddenly began to develop rare infections and cancers which were stubbornly resistant to any treatment.

HIV/AIDS is not specifically a 'gay plague' as some might believe. I suspect it was labelled in that way because it first appeared in the gay communities of San Francisco and New York in the early 1980s. HIV is spread by unprotected vaginal, anal or oral sex with a person who is infected. This can be either a heterosexual or a homosexual person. It can also be passed from a mother to her unborn child, through contaminated syringes and during blood transfusions. It should be obvious that AIDS is not limited to male homosexuals, as other people suffering from AIDS include women, babies, injecting drug addicts and haemophiliacs.

* * *

I left homosexuality in September of 1976, several years before HIV/AIDS was identified and described. I missed out on the progression of the disease and the subsequent death of friends and acquaintances. But even though I was no longer a part of the culture, I nevertheless felt a profound sense of grief that so many had died. Most of the gay men I knew were on a desperate search for love, just as I was, but at what price.[30]

I believe that as Christians, we need to balance an intelligent and informed understanding of homosexuality, with a loving, caring response to *all* people, including those affected by HIV/AIDS. This includes acknowledging and accepting that while some people have contracted AIDS as a result of their own sexual promiscuity, some have not contracted it in that way. However, to me it is irrelevant *how* a person becomes infected, as I can see no justification for judging or shunning them.

Jesus Christ personified all that was generous, caring, compassionate, kind and loving. As his followers, surely we should be displaying attributes and attitudes that are in keeping with the example and teachings of Jesus.

I grieve that so many lives have been cut short and I only feel a profound sense of compassion and sadness for the many parents and loved ones who have been changed forever by the death of a child, relative or friend resulting from this disease. When one seriously considers both the physical and the emotional pain which has been wrought by this hideous disease, I cannot understand how some people can remain unmoved by suffering such as this.

I want to conclude this chapter with a story quoted by Briar Whitehead, from her book *Craving for Love*:

> Cedar, Maryland,[31] is a wealthy upper class suburban church whose first response to the AIDS epidemic was a satisfied sense that God was judging homosexuals, and that the 'gay plague' was cleansing society of an unwanted perversion. When a homosexual man privately owned up to the pastor, also revealing he had AIDS, members of the pastoral team agreed to meet with him in a car in the parking lot once a week to pray with him. He was not invited into the church; they were afraid and angry. Some time later the young man rented a motel room and was found lying dead in his own vomit 48 hours after an overdose. A few months later a male 16-year-old attending Cedar and also struggling homosexually, committed suicide; he was afraid to confide in anyone because of the church's attitude to homosexuality.[32]

In response to these tragic events, the senior pastor at the church preached a sermon about Jesus' visit to Samaria (John 4), where he quenched the thirst of a woman at a well who was living in adultery. A question-and-answer session on AIDS before a panel of health-care professionals was also organised.

> 'If you're still having a hard time with homosexuality and AIDS after all your questions are answered, then you're up against a spiritual problem and you may need to make an appointment with our counsellors,' said the pastor. 'If you still have a problem after that you may have to find another church.'

Six months later a man called Wayne, the church's pride and joy: Christian college student president, Christian youth worker and soul-winner par excellence, stood up before the congregation to announce he was struggling with homosexuality, had AIDS and needed their help and forgiveness. There was a dead silence. Then one of the pastors rose to his feet to say he also had had a personal problem and needed the church's prayers. (He was specific later to a small group.) Then an elder rose, then several parents saying, in essence, if Wayne can be honest about his problems then we need to be too, we're needing help as well. Then a son of one of the parents stood up, 'If my Dad can open up and talk like that in front of you and ask for help then I need help too. I'm on drugs.'

Cedar began changing. In the following months several families left but 200 more arrived.[33]

CHAPTER 11

The Tenderness of God

'God wants to meet with you. He wants to have fellowship with you. In fact, he wants this so much that he is pursuing you. He does not do so because he needs you but because you need him. His is the tenderness of a mother over a fretful infant. He is there. He is speaking. And you may sit in quietness to drink in his beauty, trembling with joy.'

John White, *Greater than Riches: Daily Readings to Enrich Your Walk with God*[34]

I have often thought how difficult it is for some people to find God, especially those who only see him filtered through the attitudes and behaviour of some Christians. One doesn't have to be the sharpest knife in the drawer to realise that the church is far from faultless.

How do people see God reflected in the many stories they read and hear about sexual abuse – both homosexual and heterosexual – perpetrated by leaders in the church? In many cases this sexual abuse was covered up and hidden for years, instead of being acknowledged and some form of apology and restitution made to the victims. I'm sure many have heard the stories of the embezzlement of church funds by accountants who should have been able to be trusted. Or the exposure of high profile church leaders, some of whom have lived in luxury with money donated for the running of the churches they were responsible for. The world press has reported the story of a man who was in charge of a huge American congregation, yet led a double life for years. His public persona was one of a happily married man with children, a pillar of the church, whilst secretly he was regularly paying a male prostitute for sex.

Watching bigots parading around with placards that read 'God Hates Gays' or 'Queers Are Going To Hell' would do nothing to commend Christianity to anyone, let alone a person who is struggling with same-sex attraction and is genuinely searching for God. One can't really see a God of love reflected in these actions. It is no wonder that many in the gay community react with disgust and revulsion to some of the behaviour in the church. Christians cause a great deal of harm by voicing their prejudices publicly. Thomas Schmidt gives some excellent advice in his book *Straight and Narrow?*

> Christians who cannot yet deal with the issues calmly and compassionately should keep their mouths shut, and they should certainly stay away from the front lines of ministry and public policy debate – not to mention television talk shows. Such people are hard to reach, because they suspect that those who call them to account are 'soft on sin.' They must be convinced that the way of Jesus is the way of the Wounded Healer, not the Holy Terror.[35]

The other side of the coin is the unjust hostility many gays demonstrate towards the church. This came home to me in a personal way when the organisation I worked for had to cancel a planned conference.

Liberty Christian Ministries had made arrangements to run this conference at a large theological college in Sydney. The conference was for Christians who were struggling with unwanted homosexual attraction. It was also for parents and loved ones who had been affected by the homosexuality of someone they loved. It was never the policy of Liberty to proselytise the gay community, nor would we have ever tried to talk anyone out of homosexuality. The conference was intended to support those who had made the choice not to be actively homosexual. Some members of the gay community heard about the planned conference and immediately labelled it as 'homophobic' and 'an assault on their rights'. Advertisements in the gay press called for a picket and protest demonstration, and after careful thought by the management committee of Liberty and acting on advice from the police, the conference was cancelled.[36]

Just as some gays are repulsed by the behaviour of the more bigoted Christians, when some Christians see the offensive behaviour of some in the gay community, they decide that they don't want anything to do with homosexuals. Sadly, these reactions from both groups work to the detriment of each other.

If you are a person struggling with unwanted same-sex attraction and you are searching for God, my advice is to try and put aside any faulty, distorted images you have about God and try to see him as he really is. Go to the Bible and see what it says about the character of God.

It is in the Bible we discover the fundamental truths about God. It is in the Bible that we meet Jesus Christ, who is God's ultimate revelation of himself to us. If we want to know God, we need to look at Jesus. His character, actions and life reveal to us the character of God. Jesus Christ claimed to be Son of God and the Saviour of mankind. Some who heard him believed, left everything to follow him and, after his death and resurrection, chose to proclaim his message to the world. Others who heard him declared him to be mad.

Jesus presents us with a choice. Do we believe his claims or do we reject them?

When we read the gospels, they reveal to us a Jesus who demonstrates his unconditional love for all of us. They reveal his contempt for hypocrisy, especially religious hypocrisy; his mercy; his justice; and his selfless life and sacrifice. Even a cursory reading of the New Testament will reveal that Jesus is someone who is easy to – and worthy of – respect.

If you are someone who has been hurt by someone in the church, I would like to say to you how very sorry I am that that has happened. I am sorry you have been hurt, and I am sorry if you have been biased against God by the actions of a few. However, I would urge you *not* to make an evaluation of God based on what someone may have tactlessly said to you, or said about you.

I would suggest you form your *own* evaluation of God by your own reading of the life of Jesus Christ. Look at the New Testament account of the life of Jesus, preferably in a good modern translation of the Bible, and you will see God through both his life and his words. Take the time to read and pray; seek him, and you will find him. I can guarantee you will never regret it. For me, what became important was Jesus. The claims he made about who he was demanded a response from me, and not just a token one.

Jesus was radical in what he said. For example, speaking to one of his disciples he said, 'I am the way, the truth, and the life. No one can come to the Father except through me' (John 14:6). This means just what it says: there is *no other way* to come to God. The most important decision anyone will ever have to make is their response to Jesus Christ and his claims.

He also says, 'Look! I stand at the door and knock. If you hear my voice and open the door, I will come in, and we will share a meal together as friends' (Revelation 3:20).

We are told that 'to all who believed him and accepted him, he gave the right to become children of God. They are reborn – not with a physical birth resulting from human passion or plan, but a birth that comes from God' (John 1:12,13). No hints of rejection here – *all* are welcomed by his invitation. He goes further when he says: 'Come to me, all of you who are weary and carry heavy burdens, and I will give you rest. Take my yoke upon you. Let me teach you, because I am humble and gentle at heart, and you will find rest for your souls. For my yoke is easy to bear, and the burden I give you is light' (Matthew 11:28–30).

One *becomes* a Christian; one is not born one. It is not something that is passed down from parent to child. God has no grandchildren. Christianity is not entered into by joining a particular church, living one's life according to a particular code of ethics, or by believing a particular creed. One *becomes* a Christian. Each person has to enter into this relationship with Jesus Christ personally.

Why do we have to respond to Jesus? Why does his death have such spiritual significance?

There are many theological terms which, if one is not from a church background, can be very confusing. For example, take the term 'gospel'. What does this term mean? The word 'gospel' simply means 'good news'. What is this good news? The gospel is the good news that God in Jesus Christ has opened to all of us the way of salvation.

How has he done this? From the very beginning our sin and rebellion have built a barrier between God and humankind. 'Sin' is another way of saying that we have turned our back on God, and decided to run our lives our own way, rather than God's way. Continuing in this attitude ultimately leads to eternal separation from God. God's punishment of sin in a sense gives us what we wanted in the first place – a future without God. However, God is also a God of love and compassion. One of the most quoted verses in the Bible is John 3:16: 'For God loved the world so much that he gave his one and only Son, so that everyone who believes in him will not perish but have eternal life.'

What happened was that Jesus, who was without sin, died in our place and took the punishment that belongs to us. The 'good news' is that Jesus offers forgiveness for our sin at no cost to ourselves. What we need to do is to decide if we will accept his forgiveness. The choice is ours, and so is the responsibility that goes along with that choice. If we accept the offer Jesus extends to us, we gain forgiveness and eternal life. If we reject this offer, the price for our sin and rebellion is ours to pay. We are saying 'no' to the new life Jesus offers.

If you would like to pray and receive Jesus Christ as your Saviour, I suggest praying something like this:

Lord Jesus Christ,

I acknowledge my need of you and confess that I have fallen far short of your standards. I accept that you died in my place on the cross taking the punishment that should have come to me for my sin. I now ask you to forgive me for my sins.

(Take some time to tell him any specific sins you can think of.)

I give myself to you and ask that you would give me your Holy Spirit, as you have promised, to lead, guide, comfort and teach me about you. I choose to make you Lord of my life. I acknowledge that you are the only one who can meet my needs in every area of my life, including healing. Thank you that you have heard my prayer, Lord Jesus.

I ask all of this in your name.

Thank you again, Lord Jesus.

If you have prayed this prayer, this is the beginning of your relationship, not the end. You will now need to start getting to know Jesus by spending time with him. These times will not just happen; they need to be put aside, and you may even need to ask him to help you develop the discipline to spend this time with him each day. The best way to get to know God the Father and Jesus his Son is by reading the Bible and talking to him regularly. Start with the Gospels, and then as you read, begin to apply what you read each day in the Bible. You may find it helpful to underline any passage that stands out to you as you read. Use a modern translation, one that is easy to understand, and one that is in a readable print. Your local Christian bookshop will be able to help you choose the one that is the most suitable for you.

It may also be helpful to use a daily devotional in your time with Jesus. There are many different devotionals available, and again your local Christian bookshop will be able to help you choose one. Start by bringing your prayers to him. Speak to him as you would a friend, because that is what he is. Pour out you heart to him. Remember to thank him for all that he has done for you.

Another thing that may be helpful to you is the 'Alpha' course. This is a program for new Christians, those who want to consolidate their Christian faith or those who just want to see what Christianity is about. It was developed at Holy Trinity Brompton, an Anglican church in London, UK. It is an excellent program and is being used in many churches worldwide. If you are not in a position to do it in a church setting, which is preferable, the DVDs are available. Perhaps you may be able to do it with a friend. I would also recommend Nicky Gumbel's book, *Alpha Questions of Life*[37] .

It will also be important to connect with a church in order to grow in your faith, to be encouraged and to meet with other Christians. Pray and ask God to show you where you should go. If I were looking for a church, I would be looking for one that not only teaches the Bible but also teaches how to apply it to daily life. I would arrange to have a talk with the senior minister or pastor to see what they are like and what their vision for the church is. I would be looking for someone who is open about their own life and is approachable.

I would also try and keep it in mind that no church is perfect. Wherever I chose, I would need to give it a reasonable length of time before making up my mind whether to stay or not. I would be looking for a place to serve, even if it's something simple like washing up after morning tea.

In time, I would be looking to see what the emphasis of that particular church is. For example, if the entire emphasis is on young families, children and youth, I would probably not fit in there because I don't have children but do have other interests and needs. I would be looking for a balanced ministry in the church, where the single people, divorced, couples without children and the elderly have their needs met and also have a role in the ministry of that church.

I would be making my decision very prayerfully, keeping in mind that it would be totally unrealistic to expect that all of the goals and programs of the church would revolve around me. However, it would be completely realistic to expect some of my needs to be met.

May God bless you on your journey as he has blessed me on mine.

The service was at the same church they were married in over twenty-three years before. It was to be a rededication of marriage vows and they were looking forward to taking part in it.

Anyone looking at them would have seen an average, aging couple, a little battered and worse for wear, but some people may have been surprised if they had known some of the details of their lives.

The small boy had grown and changed.

He had held on to God ... and God had not let go of him.

APPENDIX 1

When Someone You Love is Gay

Many people experience devastating emotions when a loved one discloses that they are homosexual. The feelings may be varied and mixed. Shock, anger, disbelief, guilt, depression, denial, sadness, repulsion, relief, shame, powerlessness, contempt, pity, or embarrassment may be some of the feelings experienced.

Men and women may react differently. Fathers may not be able to talk about their feelings, whilst mothers may be unable to talk about anything else. Some people may be revolted by homosexuality and see it as the worst of sins. Many know nothing about homosexuality or its causes. The conflicting feelings can be very confusing.

Wives or husbands may blame themselves for the homosexuality of their spouse. 'Did I cause this?' 'Was I in some way to blame?' 'Was it something I did or didn't do?'

The most common reaction is grief, which, for some, can be overwhelming.

Some counsellors believe that grief has a cycle which is made up of five stages. In many cases, people faced with the death of a loved one, or indeed faced with any sort of loss, go on to experience these stages of grief. However, people experience grief in different ways. It would be a mistake to think that it will all fit neatly into a package of five little steps. Rather, see the stages of grief as a rough guide. You may or may not go smoothly from one stage to another. Your feelings may swing like a pendulum; some days will be better than others, and some people may wonder if they will survive. It hurts to grieve, and it can also be exhausting. However, grief is a healthy process, as the feelings need to come out in some way.

The five stages of grief are shock/denial, anger, bargaining, depression and acceptance, although they may not necessarily occur in this order.

Shock/Denial

It has been said that denial starts when we are confronted with something that is unacceptable. We may find ourselves saying things like, 'He can't be gay, he's a Christian,' or, 'It's just a phase she's going through.'

One mother's reaction to the disclosure of her son's homosexuality was that she thought she was going mad. She said that for weeks she had the word 'homosexual' running around in her head, and she felt as if she was in a nightmare but couldn't wake up.

Bargaining

Parents or spouses may torment themselves by thinking things like, 'If only I had done this or that, this wouldn't be happening.' 'If he would drop that friendship he wouldn't be this way.' Some people may try to bargain with God by making all sorts of promises to him if only he will deliver the son/daughter/husband/wife from homosexuality.

Anger

Anger may involve some very strong emotions such as rage. 'How dare my son/daughter/husband/wife do this to me?' 'This is so unfair. I didn't ask for this, it has been forced on me. I don't want this to be happening!' The anger may be directed towards the person, towards themselves, towards other family members, and in some cases towards God. Anger may come from feelings of disappointment, betrayal, hurt, fear, abandonment or powerlessness. Anger is not always rational, and at times it can be very destructive.

We need to find a safe way to let our anger out. I found that going for a drive and screaming helped me. I chose a road that went through a forest and so had very little traffic. Then I let it go. I felt quite foolish to start with, but it didn't take long to really get into it. I did it so well that I was hoarse the next day and wondered if I had permanently damaged my voice. I hadn't, and I felt a great deal better for having a good yell. I had a friend who once heaved large rocks at a tree. Poor old tree, but it worked for him. Sometimes physical exercise or exertion may be helpful, but whatever you choose, it needs to be a safe way of releasing your anger. If you feel stuck or find yourself turning your anger inward, seek professional help. A counsellor with experience in grief should be able to help you find healthy ways of exploring and expressing your anger.

Joe Dallas in his book *When Homosexuality Hits Home* has this to say about anger:

> This can be the most destructive of all the grief stages, so for the sake of everyone involved, be careful how you react. When you're angry, you may want the relief of an emotional explosion, and that may cause you to use the harshest, deadliest words you can think of. I've known parents who, out of their own rage, told their sons or daughters they'd rather see them dead than gay. I've heard brothers call a homosexual sibling a 'freak who oughta be strung up and burned' (I'm quoting exact words here!), and I've seen whole families reject and humiliate a gay relative through name-calling and cruel, senseless remarks. And in each case, these family members lived to regret – bitterly – every vicious word they spit out at their loved ones but can't, as much as they'd like to, retract or erase.[38]

Depression

Depression may persist for a long time; it can last for weeks, months, or in some cases, years. Isolation may occur; some people withdraw from church, family, or friends, because they just can't deal with people or don't know what to say to them.

People may feel ashamed of their situation; in this case, withdrawal is an easier way for them to cope. Sometimes they may be in need of solitude, in order to gather emotional strength.

In some cases parents may go on to embrace a 'liberal' theology, rejecting what the Bible says about homosexuality. Some may do this so as not to lose the love of their child. Others may convince themselves that God couldn't possibly object to their child being 'gay'.

Acceptance

This is the stage of grief when the pain hurts less. The sadness and other intense feelings are now beginning to diminish. A fresh trust and faith in God may be developing.

It is important to remember that people move in and out of the stages of grief. For example, if a son takes a new partner or a wife finds her husband has fallen sexually after a long period of abstinence, there will be a resurgence of the old feelings of the past.

It is important you give yourself permission to grieve. It is also important that you take as much time to grieve as you need. People close to you may or may not understand that you need time, but don't let that pressure you in any way. Be easy on yourself – you have experienced a great loss. Take the time to be kind to yourself, as the process you are in will take time. God understands what you are going through, so turn *to* him, not *away* from him.

* * *

A critical step in the recovery process is to place the loved one in the hands of God for him to work. This is vital for any parent or spouse. God is the only one who can bring our loved one back to himself and bring recovery to them if that is what they choose. It is important that God be allowed to do the work himself. Parents leaving tracts under their child's pillow, nagging the child about church or God and applying all sorts of pressure does not help; in fact, it may alienate them. The process may then take that much longer or be aborted permanently. Trust God, and let him work in his own way and time.

I have heard stories of people who were struggling with unwanted same-sex attraction being told to marry and that marriage would solve their problem. This is not only unhelpful, it is really quite stupid. Sex doesn't fix homosexuality. Homosexual sex won't fix it, and nor will heterosexual sex. If one thinks about it for longer than five seconds, one will realise that marriage will not fix abuse issues, detachment from the parent of the same sex, labelling, or any of the other things many people with same-sex attraction have in their past.

When a husband announces he is gay, the wife is going to experience a different grief and hurt from the children of that marriage. So often, the children are forgotten at this time. This is a *family* in crisis. *All* of the family need help, including the husband – if he is desirous of it.

It is important for those of you who are spouses to realise that the homosexuality of your spouse was there before the marriage. If the roots of your partner's homosexuality were not dealt with before the marriage, obviously the same-sex attraction is likely to resurface later. Many wives and husbands go on an unnecessary guilt trip, blaming themselves for the homosexuality of their partner. Reading and learning about the causes and roots of homosexuality can bring relief from false guilt of this type.

Joe Dallas emphasises this:

> Be clear about this, first and foremost: You have *nothing* to do with your spouse's homosexuality or with his or her decision to indulge it. You didn't create the problem – it existed long before you ever met your partner. And you've done nothing to make your spouse's desires for the same sex increase, nor have you had anything to do with your partner's decision to act on these desires.
>
> You are *not* the problem; you did not *create* the problem; you are not *responsible* for the problem.[39]

If your spouse has been sexually active outside your marriage, you need to be tested for sexually transmitted diseases. This is absolutely imperative:

> If you have discussed your spouse's behaviour, and the problem is out in the open, determine immediately if your partner has put you at risk for HIV (the AIDS virus) or other sexually transmitted diseases.
>
> If you're *certain* the behaviour has only involved non-contact activities (such as using pornography or Internet chat rooms), then you're not endangered. But if you are in any doubt as to whether or not he's told you the truth, or if he has admitted to being sexually active with other men, then you need to be tested immediately. Abstain from sexual relations now, and make it clear that you will be tested, and that you'll need him to do the same, before you can resume them. Make an appointment with your physician and be honest about the reason. Be tested for HIV and other sexually transmitted diseases, and follow your doctor's guidance to the letter.[40]

There will be many things for you as a spouse to consider about the ongoing relationship with your husband or wife. Do you stay in the marriage or leave? Are there children to consider? Did you marry your husband to fix his homosexuality? If so, there will certainly be issues that need to be addressed by a professional counsellor. Counselling may be necessary to begin the long sorting out process before any of these questions can be resolved. Counselling is not an admission of failure; it's just a common sense way of gaining some professional help at a time when it is most needed.

Ongoing support will be a helpful part of the process. Try not to let any shame you may be feeling keep you isolated. Love, gentleness and a person who knows how to listen can be an enormous help at this time.

Often the greatest gift we can offer a grieving person is our presence. We may not be an expert in the area of homosexuality, and we may not have any answers to give, but just being there as a friend and allowing them to express their grief – if that is what they want – will be a huge comfort to them.

Support Groups

The components of a good support group are friendship and support with others going through similar circumstances in a confidential, caring environment. This reduces isolation and shame. Support groups need time for social, teaching and prayer components.

Our experience with our family support groups was a very special one. Many participants found real comfort as they dealt with their various situations and faced the pain with God as well as sharing it openly with others. Running this type of group taught us to be very flexible and open to the Holy Spirit to lead, as we were never sure who was coming and where each person would be emotionally and spiritually.

Spiritual Growth

Spiritual support needs to be offered by the church family in the form of trusted Christian friends and pastors who will listen, share the burden and give spiritual encouragement. Family members need to nurture themselves spiritually by tucking in to the love of their heavenly Father; they need to avoid focussing on 'the problem' to such an extent that their own walk with God suffers.

Relationships

Keep communication open with the one who has disclosed. Share how you feel as a Christian about homosexuality – lovingly, biblically and *once only*. Parents need to rebuild the relationship with their child as normally as possible. The same applies for siblings with their brother or sister.

Wives have a much harder road of rebuilding trust again. This may take years and then only if the husband is prepared to seek recovery and healing.

Prayer

This should never be underestimated. Parents have no power to change their child's decision about becoming actively homosexual, but the extraordinary weapon parents *do have* is prayer, and they need to employ it in earnest. If the son or daughter is in a homosexual lifestyle and doesn't know Jesus, *Jesus* is the primary issue, not homosexuality. Pray for the conversion of the child, not that the child will become heterosexual. When you don't know how to pray, ask that God's will be done in their lives. He knows better than you what they need. The priority is for our loved ones to come to a saving faith in Christ or to come back to him if they have strayed.

We are not responsible to clean up people's sex lives. The Holy Spirit will do that when they come to, or come back to him. Jesus receives us as broken sinners, warts and all. He forgives, cleanses, and gives us a place in his family; as the Holy Spirit works in us *he* does the job of convicting, cleaning up and healing.

Pray for the whole family, that God will heal the hurting places in each heart, wherever needed.

There will always be some people who will prefer to go for support outside of their own church environment. Many feel such shame about homosexuality that understandably, they may not want to disclose about themselves within their own congregation.

A Word for Leaders

If a church will talk about, teach and demystify the subject of homosexuality, it can do a great deal to encourage openness in the people who may be struggling either with their own homosexuality or the homosexuality of someone they love.

Over many years we spoke in countless churches about homosexuality. Always after we had spoken, there were people who came to speak with us privately. These were people who were themselves struggling, or they were the mothers, fathers, husbands, wives, brothers, sisters or friends who had been affected by the homosexuality of a loved one. I can't remember one meeting where this didn't happen. People were desperate to know what to do and how to cope.

Based on our experience, I would say that *every* congregation has a person or people who have been affected by homosexuality in one way or another. Therefore it is vital that there is teaching given on the subject by the leader of the church. This needs to be done with sensitivity and love, as there *will* be people in your congregation who have been affected.

If, as a leader, you do not feel confident to do this teaching yourself, perhaps think of inviting someone in to do it for you.

Anyone involved in the pastoral care of people will, at some stage, come in contact with homosexuality. It's important that there are good resources at hand for people who are in need. A sensible start is to have a list of reliable Christian counsellors, some books or articles about homosexuality written from a Christian perspective, and the contact details of a Christian ministry specialising in homosexuality, such as those who are affiliated with Exodus.

I believe that one of the reasons the church is now divided on the issue of homosexuality is because it is a subject which has been ignored or avoided and not spoken about from the pulpit. We are now reaping the consequences of that neglect.

Support Groups

For those who may be interesting in running a support group themselves, or who are interested in learning more about them, the following information may be of help to you.

One definition of the word 'support' that I like is 'to give help, strength, and courage'. That describes what we tried to give to the people who came to our groups.

Men and women who desire to be free of their unwanted same-sex attraction need all the help they can get. Sadly, homosexuality is one of the most misunderstood subjects in the church today. Most people, including many Christians, assume that people who have a same-sex attraction have either been born that way or that they all choose to live an actively homosexual life style. Both assumptions are incorrect.

Not everyone who is attracted sexually to someone of the same gender wants to live a 'gay' lifestyle. Many Christians who approach ex-gay ministries for help are either seeking a change in their orientation or, at the very least, are seeking support in their attempts to live a chaste life according to what the Bible teaches.

It was never our policy to promise a change in sexual orientation. No one can promise that. We offered support and discipling in the Christian faith for people who were troubled by unwanted same-sex attraction, nothing more than that. Love, acceptance and encouragement to form an intimate relationship with God were the most important aspects of the support groups we ran for many years.

Expectations

It is very important that people have clear and realistic expectations of what a group is offering. It is also important that the person seeks help of their own volition and not because their parent or their spouse wants them to get help. Such people lack the motivation for the hard journey ahead.

Some approached us with the expectation of a quick fix, or at the very least, a quick 'deliverance' session. They thought that if they could have one of these sessions, then quick as a flash, their problem would be fixed. Some people believed that if they could just find the right person to pray the right prayer, or cast out the 'homosexual' demon, they would not have the problem. For these reasons, before we were able to support a person, it was vital that they had some knowledge of the causes of homosexuality, the right motivation, and realistic expectations.

Before a person was accepted into one of our groups, we interviewed them to see where they were regarding their knowledge of homosexuality as well as their expectations of the group.

What is a support group?

Different support groups offer different things, and there are probably as many ways of leading a small group as there are people willing to lead them.

The support groups we ran were places where people were able to share openly and honestly, be accountable, and also learn about homosexuality from a Christian perspective. We ran our groups over a period of fifteen weeks, and the person needed to make a commitment for that period of time. For many, it was the first time they had been able to mix with others who were struggling with the same issues.

The groups we ran were not places to meet sexual partners, and we had strong guidelines and boundaries in place to make it a safe place for all who took part in these groups. They were also not therapy groups although, hopefully, the experience was a therapeutic one.

Self-disclosure was quite intimidating for some people, especially if the person hadn't talked to anyone about their same-sex attraction. Before people joined a small group, we encouraged them to establish a relationship with a counsellor, where they could be open about themselves; it was then less of a giant leap to begin disclosing in the group.

We found that counselling was an important part of the healing process for the person wishing to deal with their unwanted same-sex attraction. Not being professional counsellors ourselves, we were not in the position to offer this to clients. But because it was of such importance, we made it a condition of entry into our groups that the person would undertake counselling for the duration of the group. This gave them the opportunity to explore, as well as deal with the difficult issues that contributed to their homosexuality, in a more in-depth way than was possible in a group situation. For example, many of the men and women who came to us for help struggled with childhood abuse issues. Others were attempting to deal with their relationship with the parent of the same sex. Often a counsellor would be able to help them with those issues.

What is needed for a group?

The venue

We chose to run our groups in a variety of places. At times we used our home, local churches, and for a time a Bible college. Ideally the venue should be a place which is comfortable, quiet, private and close to public transport.

Leaders

Truda and I led all of our groups. We did have co-leaders to help us, but ultimately the responsibility for the group was ours. The people we chose to co-lead the groups with us were people who had been through past groups. They had come to a place of being beyond the role of a participant in the group, but were not yet able or willing to run a group by themselves.

Not everyone who leads a group of this type needs to have come from a homosexual background before they can help people. Truda was a good example of this. In fact, I believe many of the men in our groups would have benefited greatly by having a heterosexual male lead the group.

The group leader needs to be able to listen well and to be able to sit with others in their struggles and pain.

Worship

We started our group with a time of worship. Usually we used a tape, although at times we did have someone who led us in 'live' worship. Worship enabled us to move our focus from ourselves to God. The songs we chose were always intimate songs, in order to encourage an emotional connection with God. Rather than singing *about* him, we wanted to encourage people to sing *to* him.

Teaching material

Worship was followed by a time of teaching. Although we initially used the 'Living Waters' program, we eventually moved to another teaching program called 'Living and Loving at Risk' by Sy Rogers. This DVD set is still available and although it was recorded some years ago, I don't believe it has dated. In my opinion it is very practical and easy to listen to. We didn't supply notes. If the person wanted to take notes, that was up to them.

Small groups

After the teaching and a cup of coffee we would break into smaller groups. These were usually, but not always, same-gender groups.

This was a time when people could share what had been happening for them during the period since we last met. Each person was encouraged to be as open as they could, and we listened to and prayed for each one.

It was very beneficial for people to share openly, as the other members of the group could see that they were not alone in dealing with various issues. The climate of openness and honesty in the group did a great deal to break the shame many people were feeling as a result of their unwanted same-sex attraction. Sometimes people would share something the teaching had raised for them, or maybe it would be something they had struggled with during the week.

I believe the most important aspect of this time was the fact that for many, it broke the isolation and fear of talking openly about their unwanted homosexuality. They realised God loved them, accepted them, and that there was a way through this.

Components of a small group

I have been asked many times about what I think is important in a small group, and I know that opinions will differ on this.

I believe the components of a good group are: confidentiality, an openness to disclose oneself, commitment to the group, honesty, accountability, affirmation, respect for each person in the group and most importantly, acceptance.

I have participated in or led many groups over the time I have been a Christian. A group can be a fantastic place to experience acceptance and growth. It can also be a very damaging experience where a person can experience the opposite. I have to say that some of the worst – and some of the most boring – groups I have been in have been Christian.

I believe the person leading the group needs to set the level of disclosure. If the leader is not willing to be open, it follows that the people in the group will not be willing to disclose.

Not everyone who joins a group is looking for a 'head' experience. By that I mean some people want a little more of themselves to be fed than just their intellects. Many people join a group to get to know and share with others, to find a level of acceptance, and if it is a Christian group, hopefully to be in a place where they can get to know and experience God and his love at a deeper level. I believe that a group ideally needs to be a place where people are growing in a number of ways. Each person should be able to communicate their thoughts and feelings and be accepted, learn new truths and strategies, connect closely with people in a safe environment, and be fed spiritually. This means that mind, emotions and spirit are all being ministered to.

Our groups were *support* groups of a specific type, run for men and women seeking to live Christian lives but struggling with unwanted same-sex attraction. As I have said, the most important aspects of these groups were that the participants experienced *love* and *acceptance* from each other and the leaders, and had a safe and caring place to share about their struggles. In this environment, they would know that God loved them and also accepted them in their struggle. Hopefully, that in turn would lead them into a deeper commitment to their Lord and Saviour, Jesus Christ. And that is where the real healing is experienced, with Jesus.

I believe it was the *ethos* of the group that mattered most. I cannot emphasise this too strongly. The program was helpful, the worship was necessary, confidentiality was vital, and boundaries played a supremely important role, but I believe it was the relationships with other Christians and the love that was experienced which made a difference to the people in our groups.

As the apostle Paul tells us in 1 Corinthians 13:13: 'Three things will last forever – faith, hope, and love – and the greatest of these is love.'

Some of the people who went through our support groups had only felt rejection and hurt from the church, so we did our very best to help them experience something different. We wanted to be able to pass on to people the clear message that God loved them and show them by example that he really cared about them.

I don't know if we always achieved what we set out to do, but that was our aim.

Prayer

The most important aspect of all we did in the groups was prayer. Praying for each person was a vital part of the group time. In fact, many people have said that it was the *most* important part of the group experience for them.

We also had friends and various people who were supportive of the ministry and prayed for us as individuals as well as for the groups. They didn't need to know any details of the participants in the group to be able to pray effectively for them.

Success

What is success? How is it rated?

People are complex creatures. Many of those who went through our groups have gone on with the Lord. Some have chosen to remain in touch with us, and some have become valued and much loved friends.

Some gave up because they saw the journey as too hard. There were also others who exchanged their orthodox view of the scriptures for a liberal interpretation. Once again, the choice was always with the individual.

Some gays claim that this indicates that 'ex-gay' ministry is a failure because some people choose to go back into, or fully embrace, active homosexuality. Of course, this is nonsense. Look at *any* recovery program such as Weight Watchers or Alcoholics Anonymous, and I am sure you will quickly see that there are many who choose to drop out. Even in the Christian church there are those who choose to leave.

This doesn't change the fact that many Christians who struggle with unwanted same-sex attraction choose *not* to go back, or choose to have nothing to do with the homosexual community. This decision is rooted in religious and moral convictions, and for many, those convictions will never change whether or not they experience a change in their sexuality.

Frank Worthen has this to say about change:

> For the ex-gay person, change has definitely come, by virtue of the fact that he has given his life to Christ, and has been 'born again'. This event has taken place regardless of his sexual orientation. No one can deny that something very dramatic has happened. His dead spirit has come to life. The Holy Spirit has come to live within his body. His viewpoint on many things has already changed. However, God has begun a work that remains incomplete. While much may now be different, changes in attitudes, desires and relationships with others, the change process is far from finished. The change goes on day by day. Even after God has completed the change in the area He is working on today, there will be areas left to be healed at some point in the future. The ex-gay can truthfully say that he *has* been changed, he is *now* being changed and that he *will* be changed. The formerly gay person, who has based his confidence in Christ, gradually discovers that his homosexual responses are diminishing and grows secure in this fact as he walks closely beside his Master.[41]

It is a fact that many ex-homosexuals and ex-lesbians live in very happy and fulfilled marriages. I am one of them. Genuine change is possible, although it is a reality that many within the homosexual community are not willing to admit.

In conclusion

I think it would be a fair comment to make that leading support groups has blessed our lives immeasurably. We have met some of the warmest, most sincere and courageous people whom we may never have met in other circumstances. Some are now close friends.

It was also difficult, demanding and tiring work, and after 16 years it was time for Truda and me to hand it over to someone else.

Were the groups an aid to people who struggled? I would say, absolutely. I so often wish something similar had been available during my own journey out of homosexuality.

Our prayer is for others to catch the vision for this type of work, and to enter into it with a passion, love and a desire to see Christ's love passed on to a group of people whom the church has neglected for far too long.

M Bergner, *Setting Love in Order*, Baker Books, Grand Rapids, MI, 1995.

J Dallas, *A Strong Delusion: Confronting the 'Gay' Christian Movement*, Harvest House Publishers, Eugene, OR, 1996.

J Dallas, *Desires in Conflict: Hope for Men Who Struggle with Sexual Identity*, rev. edn, Harvest House Publishers, Eugene, OR, 2003.

J Dallas, *When Homosexuality Hits Home*, Harvest House Publishers, Eugene, OR, 2004.

B Davies & L Rentzel, *Coming out of Homosexuality: New Freedom for Men and Women*, IVP, Downers Grove, IL, 1993.

M Haley, *101 Frequently Asked Questions about Homosexuality*, Harvest House Publishers, Eugene, OR, 2004.

J Howard, *Out of Egypt: One Woman's Journey out of Lesbianism*, Monarch Books, Eastbourne, East Sussex & Regeneration Books, Baltimore, MD, 2000.

SL Jones & MA Yarhouse, *Homosexuality: The Use of Scientific Research in the Church's Moral Debate*, IVP, Downers Grove, IL, 2000.

C Keane (ed.), *What Some of You Were: Stories about Christians and Homosexuality*, Matthias Media, Sydney, 2001.

F MacNutt, *Can Homosexuality be Healed?* rev. edn, Chosen Books, Grand Rapids, MI, 2006.

A Medinger, *Growth into Manhood: Resuming the Journey*, Waterbrook Press, Colorado Springs, CO, 2000.

ER Moberly, *Homosexuality: A New Christian Ethic*, The Attic Press, Greenwood, SC, 1983.

L Nolland, C Sugden, S Finch (eds), *God, Gays and the Church: Human Sexuality and Experience in Christian Thinking*, The Latimer Trust, London, 2008.

J Nicolosi, *Reparative Therapy of Male Homosexuality, A New Clinical Approach*, Jason Aronson Inc., Northvale, NJ, 1991.

A Paulk, *Restoring Sexual Identity. Hope for Women Who Struggle with Same Sex Attraction*, Harvest House Publishers, Eugene, OR, 2003.

D Peterson (ed.), *Holiness and Sexuality: Homosexuality in a Biblical Context*, Paternoster Press, Milton Keynes, 2004.

J Satinover, *Homosexuality and the Politics of Truth*, Baker Books, Grand Rapids, MI, 1996.

T Schmidt, *Straight and Narrow?* IVP, Leicester, 1995.

A Tylee, *Walking with Gay Friends*, IVP, Nottingham, 2007.

B Whitehead, *Craving for Love*, rev. and updated edn, Monarch Books, London, 2003.

N & B Whitehead, *My Genes Made Me do It!* A Scientific Look at Sexual Orientation, Huntington House Publishers, Lafayette, LA, 1999.

Contact details for Exodus International North America
PO Box 540119
Orlando FL 32854, USA
Telephone: 407 599 6872
www.exodus-international.org

[1] E Peterson, *The Journey: A Guide Book for the Pilgrim Life*, Marshall Pickering, London, 1995, p 13.

[2] L Payne, quoted by B Whitehead, *Craving for Love*, rev. and updated edn, Monarch Books, London, 2003, p 177.

[3] As defined by the New South Wales Child Protection Council, *Child Sexual Abuse: No Excuses, Never, Ever*, Fact Sheet 7, 1998, p 1.
It is interesting to read Jan Frank's comments on childhood sexual abuse and homosexual behaviour later in life: 'It is not ... widely recognized that many men and women who have ended up in the homosexual lifestyle were abused as children, primarily because those within the pro-homosexual community do not wish to expose the link between their abuse and their lifestyle. If there was such a connection, homosexuality could be linked to environmental causes rather than inborn predisposition, as the activists promote. In my ten years of counselling, I have found that as high as eighty percent of the homosexuals I have encountered were abused in childhood. I am not asserting abuse as the cause, but I have found it to be a major contributor in the lives of those who become homosexual.' J Frank, *Door of Hope: Recognizing and Resolving the Pains of Your Past*, rev. and updated edn, Thomas Nelson Publishers, Nashville, TN, 1995, p 198.

[4] For a more detailed discussion about sin and other aspects of the Christian faith mentioned in this section, see Chapter 11.

[5] A Carmichael, *Gold Cord*, SPCK, London, 1957, p 66.

[6] E Elliot, *A Chance to Die: A Life and Legacy of Amy Carmichael*, Fleming H. Revell Company, Old Tappan, NJ, 1987, p 365.

[7] L Payne, *The Healing of the Homosexual*, Crossway Books, Wheaton, IL, 1984, p 38.

[8] 'If you forgive those who sin against you, your heavenly Father will forgive you. But if you refuse to forgive others, your Father will not forgive your sins' (Matthew 6:14–15).

[9] M Williams, *The Velveteen Rabbit*. William Heinemann Ltd, London, 1983, pp 4-5.

[10] GJM van den Aardweg, *The Battle for Normality: A Guide for (Self-)Therapy for Homosexuality*, Ignatius Press, San Francisco, 1997, p 10.

[11] GJM van den Aardweg, p 11.

[12] St Augustine, *The Confessions of Saint Augustine*, Whitaker House, Springdale, PA, 1996, p. 11.

[13] A Medinger, *Growth into Manhood*, Waterbrook Press, Colorado Springs, CO, 2000, p 241.

[14] GJM van den Aardweg, *The Battle for Normality: A Guide for (Self-)Therapy for Homosexuality*, Ignatius Press, San Francisco, 1997, pp 113-14.

[15] A Medinger, Ongoing Same-Sex Attractions, *Regeneration News*, January, 1999.

[16] A Carmichael, *If & His Thoughts Said ... His Father Said ...*, joint edn, SPCK, London, 1987, p 47.

[17] Regeneration is an ex-gay ministry started by Alan Medinger in Baltimore USA.

[18] A Medinger, *Growth into Manhood*, Waterbrook Press, Colorado Springs, CO, 2000, pp 203-4.

[19] B Whitehead, *Craving for Love*, rev. and updated edn, Monarch Books, London, 2003, p 205.

[20] Joe Dallas writes, 'Homophobia is a word that's been cleverly used to paint anyone who objects to homosexuality with the broad brush of bigotry. It's a relatively new word, first coined by psychologist George Weinberg in 1972, and originally intended to mean 'dread of being in close quarters with homosexuals.' Thirty years later, its meaning has broadened considerably. It now is used to apply to any person, expression, or belief that does not place homosexuality on par with heterosexuality. And because it's such a negative term, like 'racist' or 'sexist', it intimidates many people from speaking against homosexuality.' J Dallas, *When Homosexuality Hits Home*, Harvest House Publishers, Eugene, OR, 2004, p 159.

[21] This widely quoted figure of 10% seems to have had its source in the studies undertaken by Alfred Kinsey, a biologist at the University of Indiana. In their excellent book, *Homosexuality: The Use of Scientific Research in the Church's Moral Debate*, Jones and Yarhouse write that 'There is good evidence to suggest that less than 3%, and perhaps less than 2%, of males are homosexually active in a given year. The rate of males who engage in sustained homosexual practice over a significant period of adult life is probably less than 5% of the male population. The rate of men who manifest a sustained and exclusive commitment to homosexual practice is certainly less that 3%. Female homosexuality has not been studied as extensively and continues to be estimated at approximately half or less than the male rates. Female homosexuality appears to characterize less than 2% of the female population. So when males and females are combined, homosexuality almost certainly characterizes less than 3% of the population, and the correct percentage combining men and women might be lower than even 2%.' SL Jones & MA Yarhouse, *Homosexuality: The Use of Scientific Research in the Church's Moral Debate*, IVP, Downers Grove, IL, 2000, p. 44.

[22] N & B Whitehead, *My Genes Made Me Do It! A Scientific Look at Sexual Orientation*, Huntington House Publishers, Lafayette, LA, 1999, p 9.

[23] F Worthen, *Helping People Step Out of Homosexuality*, rev. edn, OMF, Manila, Philippines, 1991, p 8.

[24] Part of the political agenda of some sections of the gay community is to bring about a change of attitude and acceptance of homosexuality into the church. Joe Dallas quotes gay columnist Paul Varnell who states: 'The chief opposition to gay equality is religious. We may conduct much of our liberation efforts in the political sphere or even the 'cultural' sphere, but always undergirding those and slowing our progress is the moral/religious sphere. If we could hasten the pace of change there, our overall progress would accelerate – in fact it would be assured.' J Dallas, *A Strong Delusion*, Harvest House Publishers, Eugene, OR, 1996, p 29.

[25] D Peterson (ed.), *Holiness and Sexuality: Homosexuality in a Biblical Context*, Papers from the Seventh Oak Hill College Annual School of Theology, Paternoster Press, London, 2004, p 121.

[26] C Keane (ed.) *What Some of You Were: Stories about Christians and Homosexuality*, Matthias Media, Sydney, 2001, pp 153-4.

[27] Well-known Christian author, John Stott makes this comment about the question of 'divine judgement': 'Reverting to the question whether AIDS is a divine judgment on practising homosexual men, I think we have to answer "Yes and no." "No" because Jesus warned us not to interpret calamities as God's specific judgements upon evil people (Luke 13:1-5). "No" also because AIDS victims include many women, especially faithful married women who have been infected by their unfaithful husbands, with a substantial minority of innocent haemophiliacs and children. But "yes" in the sense that Paul meant when he wrote: "Do not deceive yourselves; no-one makes a fool of God. A person will reap exactly what he sows" (Galatians 6:7 [Good News Bible]). The fact that we reap what we sow, or that evil actions bring evil consequences, seems to have been written by God into the ordering of his moral world. Christians cannot regard it as an accident, for example, that promiscuity exposes people to venereal diseases, that heavy smoking can lead to lung cancer, excessive alcohol to liver disorders, and overeating (directly or indirectly) to heart conditions.' J Stott, *New Issues Facing Christians Today*, Marshall Pickering, London, 1999, p 406.

[28] J Stott, *New Issues Facing Christians Today*, Marshall Pickering, London, 1999, p 406.

[29] J Stott, p 407.

[30] Larry Kramer, the American playwright and gay activist, wrote an article titled 'Sex and sensibility – criticism of gay culture' which was published in the gay newspaper *The Advocate* on May 27, 1997. He starts his article by talking about a book he has read, *Sexual Ecology: AIDS and the Destiny of Gay Men* by Gabriel Rotello. This is a part of what he says: 'Gabriel's book also makes the air-tight case – still considered controversial, unfortunately, rather than

undeniable – that we brought AIDS upon ourselves by a way of living that welcomed it ... we have made a culture out of our sexuality, and that culture has killed us ... We endlessly blame the government for its hideous response to AIDS. But we speak not one syllable about how we can repair the damage we have caused that brought about so much death in the first place. We do not even admit that we walked down the wrong path. We do not admit that we made a mistake ... We've all been partners in our destruction. AIDS has killed us, and while we certainly did not invite it in, we certainly did invite it in. We still invite it in. We certainly do not do everything we can to keep it out. We have been the cause of our own victimization. I know these are grotesquely politically incorrect things to say. So be it. We knew we were playing with fire, and we continued to play with fire, and the fire consumed monstrously large numbers of us and singed the rest of us, all of us, whether, we notice our burn marks or not. And we still play with fire.'

Both Christian and secular texts exist, which carefully document the studies that have been done on homosexuality and the promiscuous lifestyle of many male homosexuals. One such book is *Straight and Narrow? Compassion and Clarity in the Homosexuality Debate* by Thomas Schmidt (IVP, Leicester, 1995). In his chapter titled 'The Price of Love', Schmidt meticulously documents many of the studies undertaken on homosexual promiscuity. The statistics are shocking and make for very sobering reading. Anyone questioning or disputing the truth of male homosexual promiscuity would do well to read this book and in particular, this chapter. Even some who are openly homosexual have spoken honestly and revealingly about the sexual promiscuity within the gay community, examples of which can be found in Joseph Nicolosi's book, *Reparative Therapy of Male Homosexuality, A New Clinical Approach* (Jason Aronson Inc., Northvale, NJ, 1991).

[31] Fictional name, true story.

[32] B Whitehead, *Craving for Love*, rev. and updated edn, Monarch Books, London, 2003, p 309.

[33] B Whitehead, p 310.

[34] J White, *Greater than Riches: Daily Readings to Enrich Your Walk with God*, IVP, Leicester, 1992.

[35] TE Schmidt, *Straight and Narrow?* IVP, Leicester, 1995, pp 172-3.

[36] In the aftermath of this protest, one letter in the gay press stood out from the others and was of particular interest: '... I now expect that those who planned the picket/demonstration must be congratulating themselves on a successful tactical operation which will lend support for such tactics being used in future against groups like these whose operations we disapprove of ... It makes our enemies prone to adopt the same brainless ('stop the meeting') tactic against us when we someday decide to hold a conference. (How would we feel if they succeeded in stopping our meeting like we stopped theirs?) ... the tactic destroys any hope of dialogue; it closes doors instead of opening them, whereas an intelligent political tactic will always be one that seeks to win over one's opponents, not ridicule them into treating us with the same contempt as we demonstrate we are only too happy to throw at them. This is political action at the level of the primary-school playground' (*Sydney Star Observer*, October, 1999.)

[37] N Gumbel, *Alpha Questions of Life*, Kingsway Publications, Eastbourne, UK, 2003.

[38] J Dallas, *When Homosexuality Hits Home*, Harvest House Publishers, Eugene, OR, 2004, p 29.

[39] J Dallas, p 100.

[40] J Dallas, p 106.

[41] F Worthen, *Helping People Step Out of Homosexuality*, rev. edn, OMF, Manila, Philippines, 1991, p 5.